The Beauty and Glory
of God's Word

The Beauty and Glory of God's Word

Edited by
Joel R. Beeke

Reformation Heritage Books
Grand Rapids, Michigan

The Beauty and Glory of God's Word
Copyright © 2016 Puritan Reformed Theological Seminary

Published by
Reformation Heritage Books
2965 Leonard St. NE
Grand Rapids, MI 49525
616-977-0889 / Fax 616-285-3246
e-mail: orders@heritagebooks.org
website: www.heritagebooks.org

Printed in the United States of America
16 17 18 19 20 21/10 9 8 7 6 5 4 3 2 1

ISBN: 978-1-60178-480-3
E-book ISBN: 978-1-60178-481-0

*For additional Reformed literature, request a free book list
from Reformation Heritage Books at the above address.*

With heartfelt appreciation for …

Laura Ladwig and **Kim Dykema**

lovers of the Word of God, its beauty and glory,
deeply appreciated for their large servant hearts
by all the faculty, staff, and students
of Puritan Reformed Theological Seminary;
in a word, the best librarians a seminary could wish for.

Contents

Preface

Without the Word of God, we have no light (Isa. 8:20). Christ is our light (John 8:12), and we cannot trust Christ apart from the word of the Lord (Rom. 10:13–17). Unless we are expositing a word from the Lord, no preacher has the authority to say anything about hell, heaven, or the way to escape the one and enter the other. When unbiblical traditions reign, the church enters into twilight and spiritual winter ensues. However, the Holy Spirit unveils the word of God to men; after darkness, there is light (*post tenebras lux*, cf. 2 Cor. 3:16–4:6).

In the Reformation of the sixteenth century, God caused the evangelical doctrines of saving grace to shine with renewed brightness and warmth. In many ways, the Reformation revolved around justification by faith alone. However, no less important was another doctrine: the Bible alone (*sola Scriptura*) is our divine rule of faith and obedience.

At our 2015 Puritan Reformed Conference, a team of pastor-theologians from Canada, Scotland, the United States, Wales, and Zambia joined together with several hundred people to celebrate this most fundamental gift of God: the Holy Scriptures. The book you hold in your hands is the fruit of their labors.

In the first section of the book, we take a step back to consider the uniqueness of the Bible as the written word of God. Michael Barrett opens up Psalm 19 so that we can see how wonderful this divine gift of revealed truth is for us. Geoff Thomas reminds us that we cannot look to our opinions or to our church to give us the final word about what is right and wrong; only God has the authority to do that, and He speaks in the Scriptures. However, the authority of the Bible is often challenged, and William VanDoodewaard models how to respond to such challenges in his response to recent errors concerning the historical person of Adam.

The second part of this book highlights the attributes of the Bible in which the divine glories of its Author sparkle like diamonds. Jack Schoeman teaches us that we can have confidence in the teachings of the Bible because God has made His Word clear and understandable for us. Geoff Thomas draws us into the drama of Christ's parable about the rich man and Lazarus to demonstrate that the Holy Scriptures are fully sufficient to instruct us in the way to eternal life. Gerald Bilkes proclaims God's inspiration of the words of Scripture such that they are infallible and authoritative—the ground and triumph of our confident faith in Christ.

Of course, we must do more than admire the Word of God; we must hear it, meditate on it, and obey it in practical, daily life. The third section of the book challenges us to do precisely that. Ronald Kalifungwa presents two expository messages on clinging to the Word in a corrupt generation (Phil. 2:14–16) and allowing the Word to shape us into godly people (2 Tim. 3:15–17). David Murray shows us how to start with the heart by exploring the topic of finding joy in God's Word. Finally, I close the book with the practical exhortation of the apostle James to receive the word and be doers of it (James 1:21–25).

We are delighted now to offer you these messages in printed form.[1] Many thanks go to Greg Bailey for assisting me in editing, Gary den Hollander for proofing, Linda den Hollander for typesetting, and Amy Zevenbergen for the cover design.

If enabled, consider joining us at future PRTS conferences, held annually at the end of August.[2] Please pray for the work of the seminary, that God's Spirit would continue to fill the faculty, staff, and students with faithfulness to the Scriptures, holiness of life, and power for effective ministry.

May God use this book so that many people will look upon the Bible with new eyes, and hear the effectual voice of the Spirit saying, *tolle, lege* "Take up and read!"

—Joel R. Beeke

---

1. Audio recordings of these talks may be found at www.sermonaudio.com.
2. See www.puritanseminary.org for more information.

THE BIBLE AS THE WRITTEN WORD OF GOD

CHAPTER 1

The Wonder of the Word

Psalm 19

Michael Barrett

Why is it that the wonder of it all doesn't keep us marveling? It is so easy to get used to the most wonderful things and take them for granted. This is true in virtually every sphere of life—tragically true even in regard to spiritual matters. So much of our creed never seems to translate into the issues of life and experience. I suppose this is particularly true regarding Scripture. We have so many Bibles, so many versions. Some of us have Bibles in the original languages in which God inspired the ancient authors; most of us have Bibles in our own language. I have Bibles for every occasion—for teaching, for personal study in Hebrew, Greek, and English, multiple copies for family worship depending on whether we're sitting at the table or in the den, for church when I'm preaching, for church when I'm not preaching, waterproof copies for reading in a tree stand, and even multiple versions on my phone. Given the history of the transmission of the Bible that is stained with the blood of those who paid the ultimate sacrifice to forward its dissemination, this is no small wonder.

In the Bible, God has revealed everything that we must know about Him, ourselves, salvation, and life. He has not left anything to chance or human imagination concerning these vital matters. God's Word is able to meet our needs, whatever those needs may be. The Word of God is our standard, our rule of faith and practice: what we are to believe and what we are to do. That's our creed about the Bible, and it begs the question as to what that actually looks like in our experience.

God is not a figment of imagination or a philosophical speculation. What we can know of God, who is ultimately incomprehensible, is what He chooses to reveal. That God, the Creator of the heavens and the earth, should bend to communicate with us, the created, is amazing and should overwhelm us. We ought to be keen to heed and to cherish every bit of divine revelation. There is wonder in the Word.

Psalm 19 is one of the classic texts in the Bible about the Word of God. Significantly, the psalmist puts in bold the wonder of the Word by framing it in the broader context of communication. Since communication is two-way, it is not surprising that the psalm addresses both God's communication to us and our responding communication to Him. God's communication is manifold, and ours is to be personally submissive. This broad theme of communication develops along three lines that I want to trace in order to affirm the title of this chapter—The Wonder of the Word—and to deepen its reality in our souls. To that end, I will follow the psalmist's structure and logic in considering communication through creation (1–6), through Scripture (7–10), and through prayer (11–14).

Part of the wonder of the Word is its literary artistry. That the Bible is a literary masterpiece does not distract from its spiritual message and intent but rather highlights its beauty and contributes to its perspicuity. The inspiration of Scripture by the Holy Spirit is verbal (extending to every word) and plenary (full—extending from spelling to syntax to structure). This is remarkably so on the surface in Psalm 19. The poetics (the way the psalm is put together) as well as the lexemes (the words) point to the threefold development. Mixed parallelism and meter mark the first division, which reflects something of the multifaceted way in which God communicates through nature. Things that are immense, things that are minute, things both visible and invisible (Col. 1:16) all join together to reveal God. Significant as well is the use of the general term for deity to express God's power over the entire world.

In the second division, the parallelism is consistent and the metrical pattern is regular. This noticeable shift is suggestive of the organization and divinely reasoned logic of God's special revelation. Significant as well is the repetition of Yahweh/Jehovah/LORD, the personal name of God so closely associated with His covenant and salvation.

In the final division, the meter becomes irregular again, this time suggestive of the changing emotions expressed in prayer. Significantly, God is now addressed in the second person, the very essence of personal and direct communication. Is this not artistry? The very sight of it is beautiful and wonderful. Now to consider the message.

Communication through Creation

Theologians refer to God's communicating through creation as "General Revelation" or "Natural Revelation." According to the apostle Paul, what God reveals is sufficient enough and clear enough to make ignorance of Him both impossible and inexcusable: "Because that which may be known of God is manifest in them; for God hath shewed it unto them. For the invisible things of him from the creation of the world are clearly seen, being understood by the things that are made, even his eternal power and Godhead; so that they are without excuse" (Rom. 1:19–20). Three thoughts from Psalm 19 warrant Paul's dogmatic conclusion.

First, this creation-communication is *unceasing* (vv. 1–2). This thought is expressed grammatically in verse 1 and explicitly in verse 2. Grammatically, the fact that both verbs in verse 1 are participles in Hebrew conveys the notion of perpetualness. The participle portrays the action as being habitual, unbroken, continual. Thus the heavens are constantly declaring and the firmament is constantly showing. The word "declare" literally indicates counting out or enumerating, and the word "sheweth" refers to informing or giving an explanation. It is as though the heavens are pointing out all the information about God. From the beginning of time, there has never been a moment when the firmament has not been engaged in this communication. Consequently, there has never been an individual in the history of time that can claim ignorance of God. That's what Paul says too in Romans 1:18–21.

The opening verse not only underscores the constancy of the communication; it identifies the "preachers" and their "message." It does so with synonymous parallelism where the second line repeats the thought of the first, but in more specific terms. This kind of semantic rhyme is one of the literary wonders of Hebrew poetry. The preachers are the heavens and the firmament, the expanse of sky and space, a more specific term for the heavens. But rather than limiting the communication to the skies, it is best to recognize these terms as an example of metonymy, or more specifically of synecdoche where the part represents the whole. The heavens as part of creation here represent the totality of creation that testifies to the message. The message is defined as "the glory of God." The word *glory* refers to something impressive, one's assets that would include position, possessions, abilities, achievements, reputation, or character. All that is subsumed in God's glory is defined specifically in the second part of verse 1 as the work of His hands. What God has made testifies to how amazingly great He is. Interestingly, the chiastic structure of the poetic lines draws special attention to what creation reveals about God. Chiasm is a literary term derived from the Greek letter that looks like "X." It is a means of focusing on the middle point of intersection. In this instance, the first line ends the way the second line begins, thereby juxtaposing the general and specific designations of creation's message (the glory of God and His handiwork). The language is exquisite and the message profound. Paul sums it in terms of eternal power and Godhead (Rom. 1:20), a summary term for all the divine perfections. What Paul didactically declares, David poetically portrays.

Verse 2 demonstrates creation's unceasing communication explicitly with pointed imagery. In an uninterrupted process, one day with effervescent excitement bubbles forth the news of the day to the next, and every night makes knowledge known to the next. It is as though one day and night can't wait to tell the next all the wonders of God they have witnessed. From the first day and night of creation week this communication has sounded forth. It's not surprising Paul says men are without excuse.

Second, this creation-communication is *understandable* (v. 3). The Hebrew says literally, "non-existence of an utterance and non-existence of words; without being heard is their voice." This is a description of the manner of communication. It is speechless and silent; it is inaudible but intelligible. In other words, there are no specific language requirements or barriers to receiving this revelation. Because words are not involved, peoples of any and every language group receive the same message. There is nothing lost in translation. Since every language group has the same advantage, Paul's assessment is on target: "For the invisible things of him from the creation of the world are clearly seen, being understood by the things that are made" (Rom. 1:20). Hence, there is no excuse.

Third, this creation-communication is *universal* (vv. 4–6). The principle is stated directly and then illustrated. The psalmist directly says that the line of the heavens and of day and night has extended over the earth and their words to the extremities of dry land, referring to the inhabitable parts of the globe. There is some dispute as to whether this refers to a measuring line or a cord, perhaps a harp string, referring to the musical sound that carries over the planet. Paul seems to employ the harp string image in Romans 10:18: "their sound went into all the earth." Interestingly, he takes David's description of natural revelation and applies it to special revelation, changing the context and referent but not the thought of widespread dissemination. Regardless of how we interpret the "line," the point is clear that there is no part of the world untouched by this communication. The daily operation of the sun becomes a vivid illustration of this universality. Nothing is hidden from its glow or heat. The sun's east-west circuit affects the whole earth and the sun executes its commission with radiance, strength, and the eagerness of a bridegroom. Ecclesiastes 1:5 describes the sun as panting to perform its daily duty. Perhaps because so much of the pagan world has worshipped the sun as a god, the sun is singled out as one element of God's creation that relentlessly does its job of declaring God's glory. Rather than being an object of worship, the sun is personified as an eager servant and worshipper of God.

Creation is amazingly beautiful and wonderful in what it reveals about God. All of creation testifies to essential truths about God unceasingly, understandably, and universally. Hence Paul's condemning sentence on the human race. But since this general revelation began at creation and was witnessed initially by man in his pre-sin state, it is not surprising that it does not communicate what man in his state of sin and misery needs to hear for salvation. Man needs a gospel, and there is no gospel in the stars. The wonder of grace is that God has not left us without the kind of revelation necessary for salvation. As wonderful as natural revelation is, it puts in bold our need of a special word to lead the way out of condemnation.

Communication through Scripture

I can think of no better way to transition to the wonder of God's communication through Scripture than to cite the words of the *Westminster Confession of Faith*:

> Although the light of nature, and the works of creation and providence do so far manifest the goodness, wisdom, and power of God, as to leave men unexcusable; yet are they not sufficient to give that knowledge of God, and of his will, which is necessary unto salvation. Therefore it pleased the Lord, at sundry times, and in divers manners, to reveal himself, and to declare that his will unto his church; and afterwards, for the better preserving and propagating of the truth, and for the more sure establishment and comfort of the church against the corruption of the flesh, and the malice of Satan and of the world, to commit the same wholly unto writing: which maketh the Holy Scripture to be most necessary; those former ways of God's revealing his will unto his people being now ceased. (WCF 1.1)

Natural revelation justifies man's condemnation; special revelation points the way to salvation. Apart from this gracious word from the Lord, fallen man has no hope: "So then faith cometh by hearing, and hearing by the word of God" (Rom. 10:17). The wonder of this word is that God gave it as soon as man needed it. The Garden of Eden, the first theater showing God's glory, became the first church receiving God's gospel. Although special revelation began in the Garden, the process of inscripturation did not begin until the Holy Spirit moved Moses to write in the middle of the fifteenth century BC and ended with the same Spirit moving John at the end of the first century AD. The product of that supernatural, gracious, and wonderful process is the inspired Word of God that has been providentially preserved and is our treasured possession. Our proposition is that we ought to be overwhelmed with the beauty and wonder of that Word.

Verses 7–10 of Psalm 19 proceed from the wonders of God's communicating through creation to the wonders of God's communicating through His Word. Before we survey this section, pay attention to the parallel structure David uses in describing God's wonderful Word. It's part of the beauty. Verses 7 and 8 highlight three facts about the Word by stating a title (what it's called), a characteristic (what it's like), and an effect (what it does). In verse 9 the pattern alters a bit by giving the title and then an expanded characteristic of the Word without specifying its effect. In six propositions the psalmist sums up the wonder of Scripture. In each instance, the attributes of the Word declare its authority and the ability inherent in the Word reveals its power.

The Law

First, the law of the Lord is perfect (v. 7). The word "law" is *torah*, the body of instruction. It is the most general word in the Old Testament to designate all special revelation, not just a legal code. It is a noun form derived from the verb meaning "to teach." Whether in legislation, narrative, prophecy, or poetry, God's Word is designed to teach, to reveal what could not be otherwise known. Its characteristic is that it is perfect. This Hebrew word means "complete" or "whole." God's Word lacks nothing. This obviously does not refer to the canon since much of it was yet to come from David's perspective. But it does mean that all the issues of necessary truth had been revealed at least in seed form. But for us, God's Word is complete in every way. The canon is complete and God has spoken to us directly through His Son, His final Word (see Heb. 1).

That Jehovah is the source of this instruction elevates its importance even more. The covenant God of salvation has insured that we have what we need. His Word shows the way to eternal life as well as maps the course for daily life. Its effect is the conversion of the soul. Unquestionably, the Word is a means of grace essential in conversion since faith can only come by the hearing of the Word of God (Rom. 10:17). But the statement goes beyond that and includes much more than its connection to the initial consequence of regeneration. The point is rather that the whole body of special revelation touches every part of life. The word "convert" indicates restoring, revitalizing, or energizing. For instance, the same word is used in Psalm 23 to describe the work of the Shepherd as restoring the soul. The word "soul" is the most general word in the Old Testament referring to the person, the whole man. The comprehensive message of God's revelation addresses the needs of the entire man. In Scripture we have instructions for what we need to know about life and death. In keeping with common Hebrew logic that makes a general statement and then develops the thought specifically, this first line in this section is broad, encompassing all the specific statements that follow.

The Testimony

Second, the testimony of the Lord is sure (v. 7). The word "testimony" refers to self-attestations. What we know of God is not relative theory or make-believe; God is not a figment of imagination. We know of Him what He has chosen to reveal about Himself. We must stand in wonder when we consider what God has chosen to reveal: He is a personal God who is the creator and sustainer of all, the redeemer of His elect, the judge of unrepentant sinners, and so much more! His self-attestation is "sure." This word means "reliable" or "dependable." Whatever God says is true; it is a Word that cannot be destroyed or proven wrong. It is trustworthy.

The effect of this reliable Word is that it supplies our basic needs. The text specifically says that it makes "wise the simple." There is nothing the simpleton needs more than wisdom, so God's Word gives him just that. There is a principle here that goes beyond the specific example: that God addresses us where we are to minister to our needs. By extension, the implications are far-reaching. For those who sorrow, there is comfort; for those who sin, there is rebuke and warning; for the wayward, there is direction. The point is that whatever we need, we can find answers in the Word of God. Remember that it is wonderfully complete.

The Statutes

Third, the statutes of the Lord are right (v. 8). The word "statutes" could be translated as "precepts" or "procedures" and comes from a Hebrew root meaning "to inspect or examine" and thus refers to what God has revealed from the vantage point of His omniscience. The point is not that God has to investigate in order to discover what He should reveal, but it does emphasize that what He reveals is the product of the divine thought considering all that He knows about us and what we most need to know from Him. He knows all that is knowable, both things actual and possible. He knows all simultaneously, both macroscopically as a whole and microscopically as all individual parts. So what He has spoken from His divine oversight He has spoken on purpose with full knowledge of all our needs.

There is not one wasted word in Scripture. This is important to remember when we come to those passages that on the surface seem to have no relevance to life. When we come to those portions that we are tempted to skip over, we should ask ourselves this question, "Of all the things that God could have said, why did He say this?" Realizing that even those obscure texts are the product of His all-knowing mind should stop us short before leaving without heeding. They have to be important.

The word translated "right" means "straight," referring to the right path to take. Without God's Word we would remain irretrievably lost. The waypoints to life and safety are clearly marked. As a consequence, God's Word rejoices the heart. Rejoicing indicates the idea of being content in the inner man (the significance of heart, including the mind, emotions, and will) regardless of external circumstances. So many never find contentment in life because they are trying to find it in all the wrong places. But because God knows exactly what we need, He has recorded in His Word what we need. God will not disappoint His people when they seek their joy and contentment in Him.

The Commandment
Fourth, the commandment is pure (v. 8). This means that His Word consists of authoritative declarations, not suggestions or options. He means what He says, and it is imperative that we understand His point. Too often we hear what we want to hear, but discerning what He means is crucial. His is a living Word, but it is not a floating message that changes with time or circumstance. His intention must determine our response. I'm keenly aware of the hermeneutical debate that pits the author's intent against the reader's response. Popular Bible study groups go around the room sharing what a given passage means to them. I don't want to be misunderstood in my bluntness, but it doesn't really matter what you got out of it if it is contrary to what God intended.

The word "pure" means "clear, bright, and radiant." Simply, it shines light on the path, giving clear directions to follow. This, at least in part, addresses the perspicuity of Scripture. Even some Christians are attracted to a Jewish cabalism with all of its hidden and embedded messages as though that becomes evidence of supernatural inspiration. Bible study, then, becomes a game of alphabetic Sudoku. The wonder of Scripture is that it is divine revelation, not that it is a puzzle. The Bible is not filled with hidden codes designed to conceal God's divine will but rather revelation to communicate that will to us. Though some things are easier to understand than others, there is a message for all people to comprehend, whether layman or scholar. As the Westminster Confession explains:

> All things in Scripture are not alike plain in themselves, nor alike clear unto all: yet those things which are necessary to be known, believed, and observed for salvation, are so clearly propounded, and opened in some place of Scripture or other, that not only the learned, but the unlearned, in a due use of the ordinary means, may attain unto a sufficient understanding of them. (WCF 1.7)

This is one of the remarkable wonders of the Word. There is something about the Word that makes it impossible for the scholar to scale its height or reach its depth, yet it is sublimely clear so that any layman with the illuminating help of the Holy Spirit can understand. Significantly, this bright and shining Word enlightens the eyes (the symbol of understanding) by giving discernment and putting everything in life in its proper perspective.

The Fear

Fifth, the fear of the Lord is clean (v. 9). What a title for the Bible this is! At first glance, it doesn't appear to be a title at all, but we must remember that this is poetry, and there is more to poetry than meets the eye. We must be sensitive to figurative language, which is so common in this genre. The word "fear" is a figure of speech called metonymy. Metonymy is using one word for another because there is some association between the two words. Here, a word designating the effect (fear) is used for the cause (God's Word). Or to turn the statement around, God's Word (the cause) produces fear (the effect). In Scripture, God allows Himself to be known, and to know God as He reveals Himself produces fear. The fear of God is that awareness of God that generates awe in the heart and obedience in the walk; it affects both worship and ethics.

The format of the Psalm shifts at this point. Rather than stating a characteristic of the Word and its effect, it expands the characteristic with two thoughts. Perhaps this is because the effect of the Word is inherent in the title. The first characteristic is that it is clean, meaning "refined" or "free from any defilement, impurity, or defect." Secondly, the Word endures forever; it is eternally settled in heaven and thus imperishable. This implies as well that the relevance of the Word is timeless and universal. Is that not one of the wonders of the Word? Something that is so old never ages nor becomes obsolete.

The Judgments

Sixth, the judgments of the Lord are true and righteous altogether (v. 9). The word "judgments" refers to the record of God's decisions. The Bible is a casebook of the divine will. A casebook sets the precedence for determining proper actions in various situations. The Bible, therefore, is to be consulted in making the decisions of life. That they are true and completely righteous describes these decisions as perfect. They conform to and declare the Lord's absolute standards of what is right in terms of both doctrine and duty. It is imperative, then, to take heed of what He says.

David ends this section expressing his wonder over what he possesses in this revelation (v. 10). The conclusion that God's Word is more desirable than gold (the symbol of wealth) or honey (the symbol of pleasure) is logically appropriate. It is an invaluable treasure and sweet dessert for the soul. David certainly did not take the Word of his God for granted; it was wonderfully special. For so many hundreds of years the Bible was a rare commodity. For us, the Bible is a common possession; however, although it is common, nothing we possess is of any greater value or can match its uncommon worth. Let us be careful not just to count or display our Bibles, but let us be diligent to hear, to read, and to heed the Word that God has spoken.

Communication through Prayer

Communication is two-way. In human conversation, for one person to ignore the other and turn away without response would be regarded as rude to say the least. To ignore God's communication to us is more than a social contravention; it is a spiritual transgression. As God speaks to us, we are to listen carefully and respond appropriately. The application demanded by the Word is always personal. As wonderful as God's speaking to us is, perhaps the greater wonder is that God listens to us speaking to Him. He is a God who loves to hear and answer prayer. This final section (vv. 11–14) demonstrates the link between God's Word and prayer. Prayer should always flow from the Word. Scripture is a guide on what to pray for; it is fuel for faith to foster belief in prayer. In the light of God's Word, David acknowledges the benefits of obeying it and admits the inherent pitfalls within himself that would hinder his desired compliance. Consequently, he prays specifically for two things: personal purity and pleasing behavior before the Lord. That is the pattern for us to follow.

In praying for personal purity, he first asks for forgiveness: "cleanse thou me from secret faults" (v. 12). The verb "cleanse" indicates acquitting or being declared free from punishment. David recognizes the gravity of his crimes against the Lord, even those unknown to any other but him and God. There can be no way forward until he has the assurance of pardoning grace. But there is a way forward because God's amazingly wonderful Word reveals that the Lord is good, ready to forgive, and plenteous in mercy unto all that call on Him (Ps. 86:5). David then expresses his desire to be protected and preserved from future sins. Presumptuous sins are those insolent sins that David acknowledges would be so disrespectful to the holy God. It is always the case that the nearer one is to God the more sensitive to sin, as an affront against God, one will be. The great transgression in Hebrew is actually indefinite, not referring to any one particular sin but any and all violations of God's standards of righteousness. He prays that he might be kept from great sin. This is a big request, but the sadly unfulfilled desire of those sincerely trying to follow God's Word is to be sin-free (Romans 7). Believers universally experience the tension between the desire to be holy and the nagging presence of indwelling sin, but the way to victory over sin is clearly marked. God's Word directs us in the way of purity. Happily, we are not left to wander our way to a closer walk with God.

David is concerned not only with avoiding sin, but also with expressing a positive dedication to the Lord in his activity, communication, and thought. He wants his life to be "acceptable" before Jehovah (his covenant God), his Rock (his stable foundation), and his Redeemer (his near Kinsman). He trusts that God will always act surely, reliably, and appropriately to meet his needs. The acceptance he desires is not referring to a legal standing that he seeks to earn or merit, but refers rather to that behavior which will be pleasing to the Lord. Every believer wants to please the Lord. The wonderful truth is that God has not left His people guessing as to what pleases Him. He has revealed it in His Word. The Bible is absolutely essential for every aspect of life, spiritual, temporal, and eternal.

So let us stand in constant wonder that God has spoken to us and resolve to live in the light of that amazingly beautiful and glorious Word. It is so easy to get used to the most wonderful things and take them for granted. May that never be our attitude about God's Word. We confess that Scripture is our only rule for faith and practice; let's live like we really believe it.

CHAPTER 2

The Authority of Scripture

John 10:35

Geoff Thomas

John 10:35 says, "The scripture cannot be broken." If these words of the Son of God are true, what we have in the Bible makes considerable demands on all men and women. If this is the Word of God and if Christ is to be believed and is the judge of mankind, the Bible binds everybody to what it says because of its unique authority. They are to obey it simply because it is the Word of God. As God is its author, Scripture has the authority of God.

The Place of Conscience
There are some people who want to make conscience the ultimate authority of conduct. They say what was said to Pinocchio: "Always let your conscience be your guide." But some consciences are, in Thomas Boston's words, "too persnickety." They condemn what God's Word does not condemn. Consider, for example, the conscience of the Jehovah's Witness concerning blood transfusions. Then there are other consciences that are the very opposite and let everything pass. They allow what God's Word condemns. They are less sensitive than they should be; they are too open. Consider, for example, how the Inquisitors burnt at the stake and tortured men and women based on their consciences. Consider the conscience of the cannibal.

All of us have to educate our consciences by Scripture. The Puritan illustration of this is the sundial which will give a correct reading only when the light of the sun shines upon it. On a bright moonlit night you can find a shadow upon the surface of a sundial and read a time, but it would be an incorrect reading because it is meant to be used with the light of the sun, not the moon. The consensus of every age and the philosophies of men and their religions will cast their own lights upon men's beliefs. People behave in accord with the light that their consciences are given. The Word of God summons the conscience of every generation to the bar of its light and truth.

When Martin Luther was put on trial in the Diet of Worms (a church court) in Germany in 1521, they brought before the Reformer arguments from their traditions, encyclicals, and church decrees. Luther replied, "Unless I am persuaded by means of the passages I have quoted, and unless they thus render my conscience bound by the Word of God, I cannot and I will not retract, for it is unsafe for a Christian to speak against his conscience."[1] The Reformation was not about a free conscience, but about a conscience that had been enlightened by the Bible. As the Westminster Shorter Catechism tells us: "The Word of God…is the only rule to direct us how we may glorify and enjoy [God]" (Q. 2).

The Place of the Church

What the Roman Catholic is to believe is told to him in the clear and unambiguous answers of his church's teachings. The late Cardinal Basil Hume of England constantly defended the importance of papal authority. He warned of the danger in the fact that "the Catholic community is now losing sight of how the Magisterium, the teaching authority, operates. What matters to me profoundly is the existence of the Magisterium."[2] When hundreds of Anglicans became Roman Catholics at the time the Church of England voted by a small minority to ordain women, Cardinal Hume insisted that there could be no doctrinal concessions to the would-be converts: the Roman faith was the faith. In what would become a famous catchphrase, he put it this way: the new converts would be expected to accept the whole of Roman Catholic doctrine, not just the parts they liked—it was, he said, a question of "table d'hote, not à la carte."[3]

Two things must be pointed out. First, the tradition maintained by the Magisterium is not available to the people. A rule of faith, to be of practical use to men and women, must be accessible and intelligible. But the unwritten revelation to which Rome appeals is not

---

1. Cited in J. H. Merle D'Aubigne, *History of the Reformation of the Sixteenth Century* (New York: American Tract Society, 1849), 2:265.
2. Basil Hume, http://archive.thetablet.co.uk/article/27th-february-1993/7/basil-hume-at-70.
3. Basil Hume, http://liturgicalnotes.blogspot.com/2016/03/its-la-carte-for-some.html.

contained in any one volume. It is scattered through the records of nineteen centuries and includes ecclesiastical documents which are hidden from the common eye in numerous bulky volumes. It is clear, therefore, that it is not possible for Roman Catholics to derive from such sources an intelligent knowledge of their own rule of faith.

Secondly, the Magisterium subverts the authority of Scripture. If there are two standards of authority of equal value, the one explanatory and an infallible interpreter of the other, it is necessary that the interpretation determines the faith of the people. The Lord Jesus Christ spoke to the Pharisees and told them that they had made the Word of God of no effect through their tradition. Consider, for example, those commandments which define our duty to God. The first commandment declares that we must worship God only. The Church of Rome permits the worship of saints, angels, and relics. It does so on the basis of a verbal quibble between *latria*, worship which may be paid to God alone, and *dulia*, worship which may be paid to saints. In the second commandment God forbids the worship of images. The Church of Rome sets aside the second commandment and allows such worship. The force of this commandment is evaded by including it under the first and dividing the tenth commandment into two in order to make up the number to ten.

Again, take an example of what the Bible says about Mary and what the Magisterium makes of it. The decree on Mary of Vatican II states, "...her intercession brought about the beginning of miracles by Jesus." But if we read the story in John 2, that is not how it appears at all. On the contrary Jesus was showing to Mary on that occasion that He was sovereign in the exercise of His power as the Son of God and would tolerate no interference, not even from her: "Woman, what have I to do with thee? mine hour is not yet come" (John 2:4). What is common to these examples is that the Magisterium has succeeded in making the Bible say the exact opposite of what it is in fact saying. If the Magisterium cannot be trusted here where can it be trusted? Is not Scripture being twisted and tortured in the interests of the church's dogma and tradition?

The Place of the Bible Alone
Authority for the Christian is found in the Bible alone. But in what area of our living is Scripture the normative and authoritative guide?

How comprehensive is its authority over us as believers? Over what parts of our lives is this Word of God to regulate and control? The answer is every part. The whole of our lives as Christians and as human beings lies under the enlightenment and dominion of the Word of God. Let us examine some of these areas.

The Word of God Is the Only Authority for Our Beliefs and Theology
If I want to know what I am to believe about God, what He is like, His attributes, His purposes, His works, what He has done for me, what His plan is for man's redemption, the promises that He has given to Christians, the necessary norms for daily life, I can find the answer to all of this in the Word of God.

There are secret things that belong to the Lord, matters about which He has chosen not to give us any information, such as: "How can we know the elect before they profess faith in Jesus? How can we reconcile divine sovereignty with human responsibility? What is the date of the second coming of Jesus Christ? Why should this person's life be full of grief while another's has been green pastures and still waters?" The Bible is silent on those things, so we too must be agnostic about them. Again, the Bible does not speak on every detail of the life of the church. The Bible does not give us an order of service for worship, nor a manual for daily Bible reading, nor the appropriate size of a congregation; but the Bible does speak about the fall of man, predestination, and what we may do and may not do when a church gathers. It speaks about Adam and Eve, about hell, and about male headship, so we are never to be silent and sheepish about these matters, but must accept that these are the things God wants us to believe. Such teaching is never given to us to fascinate our intellects. It is revealed in the context of our duty as creatures, our lostness as sinners, and our gratitude as the redeemed. God does not give us truth just to exercise our intellects, but to provide our salvation and encourage a life of good works. We must grow in our grasp of the truth, our familiarity with the teaching of Scripture, and its system of Christian doctrine.

Now it is all very well for men to speak of the perils of dead orthodoxy, and that can be a real peril. There are people whose interest is not in the great foundational doctrines of the Christian faith. They are interested in the conundrum of theology. Let us avoid that.

There are people who are animated by the great controversial doctrines that divide Christians, that men fight over, and we must avoid that spirit. But we are bound as Christians to build our consciences by growing in our grasp of the content of the divine revelation. God has taken such pains to give us His Word. This is a revelation that men can understand, and it is our obligation to use Scripture, to marinate ourselves in those fascinating truths so that they become totally familiar to us. Every Christian should know intimately the doctrines which relate to the person of the Lord Jesus Christ. Each should know of the deity and the humanity of the Son of God. Each should know the states of Christ: pre-incarnate, incarnate, and exalted. Each should know the three offices of the Messiah: Christ the Prophet, Christ the Priest, and Christ the King. Each should be familiar with the doctrine of justification by faith, that is, that God has constituted a righteousness in the life of His Son Jesus Christ, that He imputes that righteousness to all that believe, and in that gracious act of justification He declares the sinner righteous in Christ. All of us should know that. It is the stuff of believing meditation. These doctrines are not for theologians. They constitute that great body of truth that sanctifies. The apostle Paul has a striking phrase at the very beginning of his letter to Titus: "the truth which is after godliness" (Titus 1:1). Why do we need the Bible? That we may grow in godliness.

Let us be careful that we are not blown about by every wind of doctrine and that we do not cling to theories that cannot bear the scrutiny of the Word of God. The Bible has the intrinsic right to correct and control us. The issue is not what I was taught as a child, nor is it some religious experience that I have had, nor is it regarding certain ideas that have been precious to me emotionally. Those cannot set the criteria for what I am to believe for the rest of my life because they are subjective and circular. The issue is what God has said, because Scripture alone has the right to control a Christian's religious thinking.

Scripture Has the Same Authority in the Realm of Ethics and Over Our Daily Behavior

What duty does God want of me? The answer is obedience to His revealed will. Where is that will revealed regarding great principles of conduct and the sanctities of life? In the Word of God. That is the only ethical rule. We have no right to detract from it. We have no right to add to it. It is the final, definitive expression of what God says is the whole duty of man. We have heard people cry that they are in a great dilemma and that the choices confronting them are very difficult. They really do not know, they say, what is right and what is wrong. They say their problems are problems of guidance. Yet very often their problems are of obedience. The ethical passages in the Word of God are among the most lucid parts of Scripture. The Ten Commandments have a grand simplicity about them. They are expounded by the Lord in the Sermon on the Mount and amplified by the apostles in the great end sections of the letters to the Romans and to the Ephesians, or, in the book of James, the whole letter. They are among the clearest sections of Scripture.

This matter of whether a woman should marry a man who has no interest in the Christian life is not a matter of guidance, but a matter of obedience to God. The Lord says so clearly in His Word that a woman's husband must be "only in the Lord" (1 Cor. 7:39). That is not a sufficient criterion for marrying someone, but it is an indispensable one. So often we make matters of our conduct problems of guidance. We plead to ourselves or to our church that our sins are not like other people's sins. Our sins are beautiful, they are understandable, they are defensible, unlike the rest. Time and time again we have to return to the authority of Scripture for guidance about all of our daily conduct.

For example, there is sex education taught in the Word of God and it is very simple: purity before marriage, faithfulness within marriage. Scripture forbids homosexual activity and even condemns homosexual desire. Matthew 5:28 says, "whosoever looketh on a woman to lust after her hath committed adultery with her already in his heart." Scripture teaches that divorce is permissible only on the basis of adultery and desertion by the unbelieving partner. It teaches that human life begins at conception and that the balance of doubt because of the tiny nature of that person during its first weeks of life must always be tilted in favor of the unborn child.

The same Word of God that commands, "Thou shalt not kill" (Ex. 20:13) also says, "Whoso sheddeth man's blood, by man shall his blood be shed" (Gen. 9:6). So the Word of God tests our ethical obedience. Are we as Christians keeping the Word of God? Are we careful to obey it when we are emotionally disinclined? Are we zealous to do what the Bible says when we lie in the depths of depression, when we wallow in self-pity, when we know that there is a duty calling us which is unpleasant and unattractive? Have we the maturity to stamp on our negative emotions in the face of our reluctance and aversion to address what God is telling us to do? There is no greater peril in the Christian life than to make our emotions the touchstone for our duties, to wait for a warm feeling to arise before we are kind to our enemies, to pause for the moment of inspiration before we pray, to plead, "God can't expect me to witness when I am feeling like this." Time and again we have to withstand ourselves and insist that, although our wills are weak and all spiritual energy has left us, we have to pick ourselves up and attend to the duties that God has bidden us do. Are we obedient enough in the face of the tremendous difficulties and obstacles that our feelings cause us? The Word of God is authoritative in the realm of ethics.

I ask you this also: is the Bible not authoritative in the small things as well as in the great? It is one of the true signs of maturity when we are paying careful attention to matters of detail in the Christian life. You remember how our Lord's commendation falls upon men and women who are faithful in little things, and it is at that point that so often we are losing the battle. It may not seem a great problem for you to be at the doors of a church at, say, eleven o'clock and six o'clock on a Sunday. It may seem a trifling thing to be in your place at the prayer meeting during the week. It may be only a small matter to remember the work of missions and to support them. It may seem a small thing to keep certain promises. But so often it is in these small things that our submission to the authority of the Word of God is being tested.

The Word of God Controls Our Worship and the Ways We Approach God
The question that the leaders of a church must ask is not what is the most attractive form of worship, nor the most moving, nor the most fascinating to the stranger who just turns up by chance. The goal is not the most exciting form of worship, but rather the most biblical. That is all. And should you think that the most biblical is boring, that is a fearful response. Are you getting weary of the living God? All you will have in eternity is God. The one concern in

thinking about true worship is how God wants us to approach Him. The goal is whatever gives God the most pleasure. That's what every congregation must strive for continually. It is not enough that we are a growing congregation or that we gain much pleasure from our form of worship. We cannot base our arguments upon the fact that our fathers worshipped in a particular way, even for centuries. We cannot plead our own feelings, or such tastes as our love of silence, or preference for a simple form of worship, or our love of ritual, or a certain kind of music. How does God want to be worshipped? That should be our only concern.

There is a vital question that God asks in Isaiah 1:12. The people in Isaiah's day were very religious with much dutiful activity going on, such as sacrifices, trampling God's courts, offerings of incense, keeping new moons, convocations, and the spreading out of hands to heaven. The Lord God looks at all this and He asks, "When ye come to appear before me, who hath required this at your hand, to tread my courts?" God views with actual scorn all this religious activity. The people had failed to ask what God's will for them was when they gathered in His name.

What is God's will for our worship? The Lord Jesus has instituted two sacraments: baptism and the Lord's Supper. Just two. He has commanded of us in Matthew 28:19 to "teach all nations, baptizing them in the name of the Father, and of the Son, and of the Holy Ghost," and there are many records of disciples being baptized in the book of Acts. Christ Himself has also given us the Lord's Supper, commanding us to "do this in remembrance of me" and to do it "till he come" (1 Cor. 11:24b, 26b), not "sacrifice this," but rather, "do this." And in Acts 20:7, the Bible instructs that "upon the first day of the week...the disciples came together to break bread." These two sacraments alone were instituted by the Son of God. Let us make sure that both sacraments are in our congregations, and no more.

There are four marks of a church outlined in Acts 2:42: "They continued steadfastly in the apostles' doctrine and fellowship, and in breaking of bread, and in prayers." Prayer is clearly given considerable significance by the apostles: "I exhort, therefore, first of all, supplications, prayers, intercessions, and giving of thanks, be made for all men.... I will therefore that men pray every where, lifting up holy hands..." (1 Tim. 2:1, 8). Paul also says, "Preach the word"

(2 Tim. 4:2). As the congregation hears the Word of God being opened up and applied to them then as one minute follows the next they are convicted of sin and repenting, thanking God for His mercies, vowing to give God better obedience, receiving new insight and expressing their gratitude for it, hearing of the sinner's plight and praying in their hearts for someone they know to be lost. So the preaching of the Word is the actual climax of worship. In the Acts of the Apostles you will see that particular emphasis is laid on sermons and on teaching of the Word of God.

Emphasis is also placed on "speaking to yourselves in psalms and hymns and spiritual songs, singing and making melody in your heart to the Lord" (Eph. 5:19). There is indeed one occasion of Christians actually singing recorded in the book of Acts. It was in the prison at Philippi where Paul and Silas were in the stocks (Acts 16:25). There is that single example of Christian praise; we cannot say there is much emphasis in the New Testament on music, but it is not ignored. These are the elements of biblical worship that God has asked of us in Scripture; in presenting that response to God we know we are worshipping God biblically and are pleasing Him.

Scripture Is Authoritative for Fellowship
The great Pentecost event concludes with the description of the young New Testament church and its peoples' love for one another. How could it assimilate 3,000 men into the 500 that were there when the Holy Spirit came upon them? We are told that those thousands devoted themselves to the apostles' teaching and fellowship (Acts 2:42). You see the picture? Outside the city walls of Jerusalem there were 300 men sitting and listening to Andrew, and he was telling them about the life of Christ, His deeds and their meaning. It is like a seminar group, and the people are full of questions, such as "Why did Jesus say that?" and "What did He mean when He did that?" They were growing together in understanding what the apostle was telling them. But there were skeptics on the fringes of the crowd and they were arguing with Andrew. They didn't accept his interpretation of the life of Jesus and were rejecting his teaching. Andrew was patient and kind with them but they were stubborn, rejecting the apostle's witness to the person and deeds of Jesus of Nazareth. Then the fellowship with those men died. There was no way that it could

continue if the apostle's doctrine was rejected. Fellowship in unity depends upon fellowship in truth. The Bible sets out the parameters of Christian fellowship.

The Word of God Has the Right to Control the Christian's Emotional Life
The Bible is a rule, not just for all those things mentioned above, but it is also a rule for our affections. My experience is the way I react to doctrine, to Christian realities, to providences and day-to-day occurrences, and the corresponding emotions which I have to handle as a Christian believer should. I am sure we have often been inclined to exempt that department of our lives from the authority of the Bible and to assume that whatever the Word of God teaches about doctrine, conduct, and worship, surely it does not deal with this mysterious and inward area of our lives which seems so inaccessible and uncontrollable. That conclusion is a very great mistake. There is clear teaching in the Word of God that a certain kind of emotional life is normative for a Christian and required by God. "The fruit of the Spirit is love, joy, peace…" (Gal. 5:22). What are joy and peace? They are emotions. What did Paul mean when he said, "I have learned, in whatsoever state I am, therewith to be content" (Phil. 4:11b)? Is not that contentment also the normative emotional condition for the Christian—joy, peace, contentment? How far astray we can be in these areas! I am not at all sure that Christians characterized by such graces stand very prominently in our circles. Do we appreciate the contribution that a man or woman controlled by these emotions makes to the life of a congregation? Do we revere members for their contentment? Do we esteem them for their joy and peace? We should. The ability to encourage and uplift the spirit of a minister and a people is extraordinary. Persons known for their joy and peace carry a fragrance throughout the whole world. We never forget them, while those who were as straight as a ramrod, but as cold and hard, leave us with very different memories. That is the biblical norm for a personality, at peace with itself, integrated not by birth, nor by temperament, nor by psychological techniques, but integrated by the grace of God and so at peace with oneself; that is no small achievement in this neurotic culture of ours. Peace with God above and with the world around results in joy and contentment in our lives. These things are not options for a Christian any more than it is an option

whether to believe in the deity of Christ, because God's prescription for the Christian reaches down into our hearts, souls, minds, and strength, that is, into one's whole psychological condition and emotional life.

Let us put it in terms of the negatives that you find in the Word of God. Think, for example, of the great teaching of the Lord Jesus Christ on anxiety in Matthew 6, and how the Lord rebukes that worry and fretfulness to which men and women are so liable: "For after all these things do the Gentiles seek" (Matt. 6:32). The Lord analyzes it and shows how incompatible it is with a life of trust in God. Jesus Christ is virtually saying to us, "Either faith or anxiety—you cannot have both." Remember how the Lord stands before Elijah's depression and addresses him under the juniper tree, saying, "What doest thou here, Elijah?" (1 Kings 19:9b). He stands before David's despondency and says to him by His Spirit, "Why art thou cast down, O my soul?" (Ps. 42:5). He stands before Cain and says, "Why art thou wroth? And why is thy countenance fallen?" (Gen. 4:6).

God's Word challenges depression. How can a Christian be continually depressed when he believes God has put everything that touches our lives, whether in the greatest way or in the slightest way, to be under obligation to work together for our good? How can a Christian be characteristically melancholic while he is testifying to the world, "I have a loving Shepherd who sits at the right hand of God, who is in control of my life, who makes all grace to abound always to me in every circumstance, from whose love I am never, ever going to be separated!" How can a Christian who believes that message crack the moment something goes against him and be so affected that he loses his peace and joy? The Savior has asked, "Why take ye thought?" (Matt. 6:28a), that is, why worry? "Sufficient unto the day is the evil thereof" (Matt. 6:34). It is folly for us Christians who trust in a loving Father to dwell on all the possible things that might happen to us! It is so desperately unbelieving, and simply sub-Christian for us to behave in that way.

Think again of the teaching of our Lord Jesus about phobias and how He so often confronts the disciples, asking, "Why are ye fearful, O ye of little faith?" (Matt. 8:26). They are in a storm, but He is with them. The covenant of grace made flesh is there in the boat in the same storm as they are. What moral right do they have to be afraid?

Hasn't Christ said, "Let not your heart be troubled: ye believe in God, believe also in me" (John 14:1)? Why, then, this feeling that you are useless? Why do you think like that? Why this belief that nobody loves you? How can you entertain thoughts like that as a Christian when you are the apple of God's eye?

The Word of God has the right to stand in judgment over my convictions, theology, worship, and fellowship. The living Word can challenge my emotions. Only Scripture has that right, although it does much more. It looks at us in our depression, fear, worry, and discontentment so very tenderly. God deals with us like a father pitying his children. How weak and ignorant we are. He understands our frailty. With what a benign and kindly eye God views us when from weariness we have fallen asleep at the time the Lord has asked us to watch and pray. "Sleep on now, and take your rest: it is enough, the hour is come" (Mark 14:41). How long-suffering the Lord is with Job. When with such bitterness of soul Job blurts out his frustration with God and speaks so foolishly, God comes and lifts Job up and restores him to usefulness and blessing.

Nothing can help us cope with our emotional problems like the Bible can. Don't ever put yourself down because you seem to be failing to overcome a painful shyness, or because of a depression that doctors and pharmacists are trying to cure, or because of a worrying disposition, or because of irrational phobias and anxieties. God not only bears with people like that, but has used them in great ways. David Brainerd was an extraordinary evangelist, and William Cowper was one of the greatest of all hymnists. Both suffered from melancholy. B. B. Warfield's wife was an invalid throughout their marriage, but her husband's care for her did not prevent his being an eminent defender of the Christian faith. It might even have enriched it.

Conclusion
The Word of God comes in all its rich divine authority and scrutinizes our lives, challenging them, encouraging us, and helping us to believe the truth. Through this we find love, joy, peace, contentment, and deliverance from despair. There is no secret to living the "Happy Christian Life." Know the Bible. Sit at the feet of this Wonderful Counsellor and have Him speak to you and challenge you... then do what He has said.

CHAPTER 3

Challenges to the Word: A Case Study on Adam

2 Peter 2:1

William VanDoodewaard

The first challenge to Genesis occurred long before it was written. As Adam and Eve enjoyed all that God had given them, the seemingly innocuous question was raised: "Did God really say?" The questioning did not stop there; it is still a global reality. Satan still actively opposes God, hating His Word and the faithful proclamation of it. Fallen humanity joins him in his enmity. Just as in Genesis, challenges to the Word are not only external to the church; they also arise within. The apostle Peter soberly reminds us that just as false teachers arose during the days of the Old Testament, so they will be among us: "But there were false prophets also among the people, even as there shall be false teachers among you" (2 Pet. 2:1a).

Among the continued assaults against the Word is today's continued questioning of the meaning of Genesis—not only the time and manner of the origins of the cosmos, the earth, plants, and animals— but the origin and existence of Adam and Eve as Genesis describes. Most crucially for the church, this determined, continued questioning arises within self-identified evangelical Christians and is promoted by Christian publishers. These scattered Christian college and seminary professors have not only gained publishing support, but have also found a shared voice through the Biologos Foundation, an organization dedicated to re-envisioning Genesis. Propelled by the funding of the Templeton Foundation, Biologos supplies millions of dollars for research grants, writing projects, and speaking tours aimed directly at evangelical constituencies around the globe.

God's Word on Adam and Eve
Before considering the historical background and nature of this rising challenge to the Word, it is helpful to reflect again on the

God-given revelation of our origin. The opening words of Genesis describe an incredible reality: "In the beginning God created the heaven and the earth" (Gen. 1:1). The subsequent narrative unfolds in the same way. It tells us that God spoke created reality into existence: "And God said, Let…" (Gen. 1:3, 6, 9, 11, 14, 20, 24). It tells us that this took place across a chronological sequence of days, each having an evening and morning of an ordinary duration as marked by the sun's ruling over the day (Gen. 1:5, 8, 13, 19, 23, 31). Accommodating His work to the space of the days He creates, God makes a marvelously beautiful, complex creation. During the sixth day, God speaks the rest of creation into existence and function. After creating land animals according to their kinds, "God said, Let us make man in our image, after our likeness: and let them have dominion over the fish of the sea, and over the fowl of the air, *and over the cattle, and over all the earth… So God created man in his own image, in the image of God created he him; male and female created he them* (Gen. 1:26–27, emphasis added). We further read that "God blessed them" and called them to "be fruitful, and multiply" and to exercise stewardship and dominion over the earth (vv. 28–29). The passage declares that as God surveyed His handiwork he declared it all "very good," and that His creation of man and woman, male and female, occurred within the span of the sixth day.

As we turn to chapter 2, the Word brings us to focus in richer detail on the marvelous, intimate manner in which God created Adam and Eve, placing them in relationship with Himself and in a context that was in every way suited to his flourishing. Genesis 2:7 tells us that "the LORD God formed man of the dust of the ground, and breathed into his nostrils the breath of life; and man became a living soul." God then placed man in a region of His creation that was specially prepared for him: the garden of Eden. Yet, as this expanded account of the sixth day narrates, there was still something incomplete in God's activity, something planned but not yet fulfilled: "And the LORD God said, It is not good that the man should be alone; I will make him an help meet for him" (v. 18). And He does: "And the LORD God caused a deep sleep to fall upon Adam, and he slept: and he took one of his ribs, and closed up the flesh instead thereof; and the rib, which the LORD God had taken from man, made he a woman, and brought her unto the man" (vv. 21–22). Adam's response is full of wonder and gratitude: "This is now bone of my bones, and flesh of my flesh: she shall be called Woman, because she was taken out of Man" (v. 23). Moses records that this beginning of humanity is also the beginning of marriage, and there was no sin or shame in their original created state. This is what Scripture declares about our origin.

As we look beyond these early chapters of Genesis we see a comprehensive unity in the biblical testimony to human origins. The genealogy of Genesis 5 begins with Adam. In Exodus 20 we are reminded that God created man and the rest of His creation "in six days." First Chronicles provides another genealogy through the post-exilic period, also beginning with Adam. Job calls on the Lord, acknowledging Him as his Creator (Job 10:8). In return God calls Job to "Behold now behemoth, which I made with thee" (Job 40:15). Psalm 148 calls all creation to praise the Lord, "for he commanded, and they were created" (v. 5). Ecclesiastes reminds us "all are of the dust, and all turn to dust again" (Eccl. 3:20). In Isaiah, God states regarding man, "I have formed him; yea, I have made him" (Isa. 43:7). In Jeremiah God tells us, "I have made the earth, the man and the beast that are upon the ground, by my great power and by my outstretched arm..." (Jer. 27:5). Malachi the prophet calls us to reflect on the reality that we all have one Father: "Hath not one God created us?" (Mal. 2:10). This Old Testament testimony flows seamlessly into the New. Jesus, speaking on marriage as recorded in the Gospels of Matthew and Mark, states, "Have ye not read, that he which made them at the beginning made them male and female, and said, for this cause shall a man leave father and mother, and shall cleave to his wife: and they twain shall be one flesh?" (Matt. 19:4–5; see also Mark 10:6–7). As He does, He draws directly on the content of Genesis 1 and 2. The Gospel of Luke begins its genealogy of Jesus at Adam (Luke 3:38).

The fact that Adam stands at the head of the human race is one which the apostle Paul expounds by the Spirit. At Mars Hill, Paul proclaims to the pagan Athenians that God is the one who "giveth to all life, and breath, and all things; and hath made of one blood [one man] all nations of men to dwell on all the face of the earth" (Acts 17:25–26). The epistle to the Romans declares the reality of sin and death in Adam, and life in Christ. Through the "one man" Adam, sin entered the world (Rom. 5:12); death entered through sin, and so death spread to all sinners. It is clear that for Paul, Adam the first man is an essential historical reality, just as Jesus Christ the second Man is. First Corinthians expresses the same truths. In chapter 11 as he addresses worship and order in the church, Paul draws on the creation order of Genesis 2, stating that man was not created for the woman, but woman for the man: "For as the woman is of the man, even so is the man also by the woman; but all things of God" (v. 12). We find an even more explicit reference to Adam in chapter 15, with its statement of the reality that as in Adam all die, even so in Christ shall all be made alive. Near the end of the chapter, the apostle states, "And so it is written, the first man Adam was made a living soul; the last Adam was made a quickening [living] spirit.... The first man is of the earth...the second man is the Lord from heaven" (1 Cor. 15:45, 47). The pastoral epistle to Timothy again affirms the historical reality of Genesis: "For Adam was first formed, then Eve" (1 Tim. 2:13).

The final books of the New Testament continue to reaffirm the Genesis account of human origins, displaying the unity of the whole of Scripture. Jude, warning against false teachers, tells us that Enoch, "the seventh from Adam," prophesied about these men (v. 14). And then the book of Revelation, with its warnings and encouragements from the risen, ascended Christ, again reminds us that God created all things: by His will they exist and were created (Rev. 4:11).

As we survey God's Word from Genesis through Revelation, there is no exegetical or theological reason to believe anything other than that God specially created Adam and Eve as the first humans on the sixth day of creation, Adam from the dust of the ground and Eve from Adam's rib. Nowhere in Scripture do we receive exegetical cues of lengthy processes involved in Adam's origin, nor does Scripture indicate any predecessors or ancestors to Adam and Eve. They are humanity's first parents.

Did God Really Say?

Despite this clarity in Scripture, it is no surprise when fallen men echo the words in the Garden: "Did God really say?" The question of whether God intended us to understand the Genesis account literally as the account of our origin was already asked by scholars in the Jewish community prior to Jesus' earthly ministry. In fact, the challenge to the Genesis account of our origins goes further back:

extant pagan accounts of origins in the ancient Near East (Sumer, Akkad, Babylonia, Egypt, and early Greece) are among the earliest iterations of the distortion and rejection of the truth of God's creative work. As Carl F. H. Henry stated, "the tendency of [comparative religion] scholars to minimize the differences between Genesis and non-biblical so-called 'creation accounts' found in other religions of the ancient Near East must not be allowed to obscure very real and important dissimilarities.... The Genesis account confronts and challenges [them]."[1]

Scripture's internal testimony is consistent whether through Moses, the chronicler, the psalmists, the prophets, or the apostles. As the Spirit led, all wrote and understood in human origins according to Genesis. Nonetheless, while some extra-biblical Jewish writings indicate a literal understanding of Genesis on human origin, others do not. Philo of Alexandria (c. 25 BC–AD 50), a Hellenistic Jewish philosopher, wanted to reconcile Greek philosophy with the Old Testament and Jewish writings. His passion was the pursuit of an intellectually compelling view of Judaism in the Greco-Roman world—one more compatible with Greco-Roman natural philosophy. As a result, Philo proposed an allegorical approach, arguing that Genesis on origins should not be taken literally. According to Philo, the "days" did not refer to time. He argued that Genesis was an allegory; the heavenly man was created first, and later the material, earthly man.

Philo's approach was starkly different from the contemporary New Testament approach to Genesis, in which nothing of this sort is intimated, but instead there is complete coherence with a literal reading. From before Philo and after, many Greek and Roman intellectuals viewed their Greco-Roman, religious-historical "origins" texts—represented by *Iliad*, *Odyssey*, and *Aeneid*—as crude, barbaric, primitive, and embarrassing to accept literally. The new, popular philosophies propounded an ancient, near eternal earth; elevated the spiritual over the material; and adopted more philosophical, allegorical readings of their writings. Not surprisingly, they scoffed at the Old Testament account of origins believed by Christians and many Jews. This intellectual criticism by the scholars and thinkers of the

---

1. Carl F. H. Henry, *God, Revelation, and Authority* (Waco, Tex.: Word Books, 1983), 6:109.

day viewed Genesis as primitive—not worthy of believing at face value. It was a significant cultural pressure. Where Greco-Roman society and culture looked at Genesis and responded by saying, "God did not do this," some early Christians began to wonder, "Did God really say?"

Among those who sought a middle way were Clement and Origen in Alexandria. They did so drawing on Philo. Feeling the ongoing intellectual criticism of Genesis in their culture, they turned to echo the culture. Origen sought to find a "deeper meaning" in the text, "deeper" than its "plain reading," criticizing those who held to a "superficial interpretation…by saying that the creation of the world happened during a period six days long."[2] Instead, in line with prevailing neo-Platonism, he argued that creation was a temporal expression of an eternal order, concluding that there was a two-stage creation, the latter stage happening in one, simultaneous act. God merely presented it to us in a sequential, six-day form to accommodate Himself to our understanding. Being the intellectual he was, Origen himself had gotten beyond this and no longer needed such an accommodation.

The views of the allegorists within the early church would resurface in new guises. Subsequent iterations claimed new, deeper insight into Genesis 1 and 2, arguing that a plain reading of the text was beneath the dignity of anyone intelligent. Origen's alternative allegorical, neo-Platonic hermeneutic on Genesis 1 was carried along into Genesis 2: just as there was first an eternal, spiritual order, so also Adam was pre-existent outside of time and material creation in his spiritual being, as was Eve; they were subsequently materially created by God from the dust and from the rib.

Did the entire early church follow this reinterpretation? While some did, many did not: Clement of Rome, Justin Martyr, Theophilus of Antioch, Irenaeus, Tertullian, and Hippolytus of Rome all held to the literal reading of the text, rejecting Origen's approach. As we walk through the writings of the early church fathers in the following centuries, it soon becomes clear that the literal understanding remained strong. Many continued to believe that God created Adam and Eve, from the dust and the rib, body and soul, on the sixth day,

---

2. Origen, *Contra Celsum* (Cambridge, UK: Cambridge University Press, 1980), 375.

with no prior existence. But there were also continued, constant challenges—both from outside the church and from within.

Moving into medieval European church history—despite the strong influence of Augustine, who followed Origen—there remained a steady stream of those who propound the literal reading of creation and human origins. English theologian Bede criticized Augustine and Origen for teaching "by a loftier scrutiny that everything which they read concerning the first seven days is of necessity otherwise than the custom of our age holds," noting that "equally Catholic Fathers like Clement of Rome, Ambrose, Basil, and Jerome all held to a six day creation."[3] Expounding Genesis 2:7 in relation to Genesis 1:26–27, Bede declared,

> Here, then, is described at greater length the making of man, who was indeed made the sixth day; but there his creation was mentioned briefly which here is expounded more fully, namely that he was fashioned into the substance of body and soul. Of these the body was formed of the mud of the earth, but the soul was created out of nothing by the inspiration of God; but also the woman was fashioned from his side while he slept.... He breathed into his face the breath of life, and man became a living soul, when he created for him the substance of the soul and spirit by which he would live.[4]

Bede rejected the two-stage creation of man. What is perhaps most remarkable about the medieval era is that despite the penchant for allegorizing seen in the works of writers like Aquinas, an abiding stream of the literal tradition continued. While many asked about origins, "Has God really said," by grace there were also many who replied, "Yes, He has."

With the transition from the Medieval to the Reformation era came the end (at least among Protestants) of the allegorizing abandonment of the creation account. Remarkably, instead of the continuance of two long-held streams of thought in the church, one was utterly extinguished. From William Tyndale to Martin Luther and Philip Melancthon, Ulrich Zwingli, Heinrich Bullinger, Wolfgang

---

3. Bede, "The Day," in *The Reckoning of Time*, trans. Faith Wallis (Liverpool, UK: Liverpool University Press, 1999), 19–21.

4. Bede, *On Genesis*, trans. Calvin Kendall (Liverpool, UK: Liverpool University Press, 2008), 109–110.

Musculus, and John Calvin to Peter Martyr Vermigli and countless others, there was a wholesale return of the church to a literal reading of Genesis.

Why? There were two reasons. First, they pursued what we call a historical-grammatical reading of the text, deeply valuing a recovery of the literal sense of it. Second, the Reformers believed that the text was the interpreter of created reality. In other words, they believed that Genesis set the parameters for natural philosophy, not the other way around. One of Calvin's students, Lambert Daneau (c. 1530–1595), who later served as professor of theology at both Geneva and Leiden, argued,

> As it is to be granted that [Moses] spoke simply, so it cannot be proved that he spoke or wrote lyingly, falsely and ignorantly of those things.... [He spoke] simply but truly, barely but rightly, commonly but purely.... Some are of the opinion that all those things which he wrote in the first chapter of Genesis are to be interpreted allegorically. So neither do they think those six days are the space of time, neither indeed that the woman was made from Adam's rib.... Which opinion if it be true, what shall be sure or certain in all that whole chapter, and such like writings of other prophets, as appertaining to the knowledge of natural philosophy...? Shall we say, against the assured faith of Scripture that any one of the chiefest philosophers, to wit, Plato or Aristotle, which were heathen men, were called by God to counsel when he went about framing and creating the world, that they should know more than Moses the servant of God, whom God himself taught, and showed unto him such things as he should commit to writing...and especially for the instruction of his most dearly beloved church? Surely this cannot be taught, much less spoken, without notorious blasphemy against God himself.[5]

Whether Lutheran, Anglican, Dutch Reformed, Presbyterian, or Huguenot, it appears that for a significant season well into the post-Reformation era Protestantism recovered and unanimously championed the historical Adam and Eve of Genesis, specially

---

5. Lambert Daneau, *The Wonderfull Woorkmanship of the World Wherin Is Conteined an Excellent Discourse of Christian Naturall Philosophie*, trans. Thomas Twyne (London, 1578), 9–10.

created by God on the sixth day. This was also the case beyond the days of the Westminster Assembly among English Puritans. So it is no surprise that when we look to the Reformed confessions and catechisms we see a literal, plain reading approach to Genesis, taking it at face value. The Westminster Larger Catechism provides an example of this pattern:

Q. 15. What is the work of creation?

The work of creation is that wherein God did in the beginning, by the word of his power, make of nothing the world, and all things therein, within the space of six days, and all very good.

Q. 17. How did God create man?

After God had made all the other creatures, he created man, male and female; formed the body of the man out of the dust of the ground, and the woman of the rib of the man, endued them with living, reasonable, mortal souls; made them after his own image, in knowledge, righteousness, and holiness, having the law of God written in their hearts, and power to fulfill it, and dominion over the creatures, yet subject [able] to fall.[6]

The unanimity on Genesis and human origins was not to last long. In fact, among Socinians, occultists, and skeptics, the old stream of Genesis criticism and reinterpretation continued, under the influence of natural philosophies rooted in Greek thought and at times with a new spin.

Already in the 1530s, Swiss physician, astrologer, and occultist Philip von Hohenheim suggested that islands just being discovered by Europeans "were populated by people which are from a different Adam."[7] He specifically stated that African pygmy peoples were not of Adamic descent, and might even lack language and souls, and so might not really be human. Jacob Palaeologus, a Roman Catholic turned Socinian, actively promoted the idea that Adam and Eve were not the ancestors of all people in a 1570 tract—fifteen years prior

---

6. Westminster Larger Catechism, Q. 15, 17.

7. Paracelsus [Philippus Aureolus Theophrastus Bombastus von Hohenheim], *Astronomia Magna: oder Die gantze Philosophia sagax der grossen und kleinen Welt des von Gott hocherleuchten erfahrnen und bewerten teutschen Philosophi und Medici Philippi Theophrasti Bombast, genannt Paracelsi magni,* Frankfurt: Sigismund Feyerabend, 1571, 8–9.

to being executed in Rome for heresy. Giordano Bruno, a Dominican friar turned Renaissance free-thinking skeptic, drew on medieval Jewish occult (Kabbalist) and Chinese sources to hypothesize that Indians and Africans had "other" origins, stating that they were "not of human generation." Sir Walter Raleigh's company of explorers included the astronomer and mathematician Thomas Harriot who taught that the natives of North America had origins predating Adam by as much as ten thousand years according to their own histories.

This fringe—which had some influence in high society in Protestant nations—made its first significant challenge against the Protestant recovery of Genesis in 1655, through the writings of Isaac La Peyrere. La Peyrere had been born into a French Huguenot family of Jewish origins; he was fascinated by Judaism and exemplifies the connections between Renaissance and early Enlightenment. His book *Men Before Adam* follows a line of Jewish occult thought which argued that only the Jews were Adam's descendants. La Peyrere's conclusion was that Scripture only intended to tell the Jews' history; Gentiles had other origins. Placing a greater weight of authority in pagan chronologies than Scripture's genealogical chronologies, La Peyrere surmised that man must have preexisted the "Jewish Genesis" by tens of thousands of years.

La Peyrere was vigorously countered by many orthodox Reformed theologians: Francis Turretin, Herman Witsius, and leading English Puritans were among those who stood to defend the Genesis account of origins. However, his thought and challenge to Genesis did gain some ground, especially within the Church of England, with its wide latitudes under Charles II and following monarchs.

Springing from ancient critiques, the headwaters of the modern challenge to Genesis flowed through La Peyrere's thought joining with ideas of thinkers like Spinoza, Newton, Voltaire, and Kant. Each viewed the Genesis account as primitive and rudimentary, calling for the development of a new, natural philosophy drawing on ancient Greek and other approaches to origins. Charles Darwin's family stood in this line. Like his grandfather, he believed that "the Old Testament from its manifestly false history of the world…was no more to be trusted than the sacred books of the Hindoos, or the beliefs of any barbarian."[8] Darwin sought to develop a philosophical alternative to Scripture that would show how "mother earth" gave birth first to "creatures of less purposive form," which then led to others "with greater adaptation," answering Immanuel Kant's call to pursue this "daring venture of reason."[9]

With the scientific advances of the nineteenth century came great optimism in philosophy, science, and human ability. Evolutionary models for origins became popular and began to make deep inroads into the church. Swayed by the acceptance of the new natural philosophy in intellectual circles, more and more Protestants began to ask, "Has God really said?" Resurgent teachings of an ancient earth caused doubt that God created everything in six days; evolutionary theories caused doubt that God created with immediacy in an awesome display of His power and wisdom. God's work and the origin of humanity, as God describes in His Word, is the focal point of the challenge.

Otherwise sound Protestant theologians, like B. B. Warfield, sought a middle way by creating a synthesis of the Genesis account and the new natural philosophies, though voicing some criticisms of the latter. But others viewed these attempts at synthesis as a repeat of an age-old error. To give up the plain reading of early Genesis was to give away Scripture's authority and clarity on beginnings, as Warfield's colleague and friend Geerhardus Vos argued. In some Protestant denominations, openness to theistic evolutionary models became acceptable. Belief that God's work of creation spanned eons, using natural processes with perhaps an occasional supernatural intervention, meant that God became more distant, less perceptible in His activity. For such Protestants, in the realm of origins God became a distant first-cause, or one who ethereally hovered over and directed what appeared an essentially self-directive process.

The impacts of this increasing questioning of the historic understanding of the Genesis account of creation were not merely issues of time. The shift away from the historic, literal understanding of Genesis on origins put immediate pressures on the account of Adam and

---

8. Nora Barlow, *The Autobiography of Charles Darwin 1809–1882* (London: Collins, 1958), 86–87.

9. Immanuel Kant, *Critique of Judgement*, trans. J. H. Bernard (London: MacMillan, 1914), 340.

Eve. Among increasing numbers of intellectuals, two options came into favor: either there was no Adam, or there was an "evolved," historical Adam. Those who held to the latter were necessarily forced to posit that somewhere along the evolutionary line God made a distinction: God created material man first, then later made him a spiritual man. Ironically, the error was a reversal of the ancient allegories: they had prioritized the spiritual over the material, and now the material had taken precedence over the spiritual. The two modern options of either no Adam or an evolved Adam would prove devastating, bringing with them significant doctrinal and practical consequences.

From the nineteenth century to the present day, varied forms of the same critical arguments against Genesis have come to each generation of the Protestant church. Yet God has met them ably; He has preserved a steady stream of those who continue to hold to a clear, authoritative Genesis, declaring a profoundly supernatural work of creation.

What Difference Does It Make?

While this brief historical sketch illustrates the history of a faithful exposition of Genesis and the nearly constant challenges to it, a pressing question remains: what difference does it make? What are the theological and practical implications of departing from a Genesis understanding of human origins, as plainly presented in the text? There are key differences between holding to a literal Genesis view of human origins, and non-literal, evolutionary views.[10]

Scripture and Hermeneutics

If you hold to the literal reading of Genesis 1 and 2, it necessarily means that God created Adam and Eve from the dust and a rib on the sixth day. They are the first humans without ancestry. Holding to this does not negate the literary beauty and structure of these chapters. Rather it enables rich reflection on these realities and their subsequent unfolding throughout Scripture. The literal tradition harmonizes seamlessly with the wider themes of Scripture it connects

---

10. For a more extensive engagement with these differences see William Van Doodewaard, *The Quest for the Historical Adam* (Grand Rapids: Reformation Heritage Books, 2015), 281–312.

to: the Garden, the Temple, Christ's person and work, the final day, and the inauguration of the new heavens and new earth.

The literal reading of the text is entirely cohesive with every other Old and New Testament reference to creation and human origins. We understand that God acts supernaturally, miraculously, above and beyond the natural. We see that He intervenes in the ordinary processes and principles of the created order that He created, sustains, and rules. It is consistent with Christ's resurrection and the prophecy of His second coming. The literal tradition also connects with a high view of the authority and clarity of Scripture as the interpreter of creational and human existence. This is necessary for us due to the noetic effects of sin: our fallen inability to assess appropriately creational and human existence by general revelation.

By contrast, when we adopt an alternate approach to the text with the need to read things in a figurative manner (usually beginning with the days), we adopt a hermeneutical principle that is erosive. It is erosive because the text is not meant to be interpreted in a figurative manner, so when we adopt this approach there is no textual, exegetical reason for an end-point of its use. We may decide that we would like to stop with figurative days, maintaining a special creation of Adam and Eve as some proponents of the framework hypothesis do, but that is merely a personal decision: there is no exegetical or textual ground for doing so. So many other framework hypothesis proponents sail on through the text: the dust becomes figurative, the rib becomes figurative, Adam and Eve themselves simply become figurative for humanity. On it goes, through the fall and beyond.

Those who advance further in their new hermeneutics note that they are simply being consistent in their exegetical approach—and they are pursuing consistency. But it is a devastating consistency which has every reason to go on to erode the entirety of the teaching of the Word of God.

Man and the Ethics of Human Life

The millennia-long battle over our origin is about you, about us. Are you an evolved animal? Were your ancestors primates? Or did God intimately and specially create you uniquely in His image? The literal understanding holds to a marvelous distinction between man and animals: Each animal is created according to its kind. God says,

"Let us make man in our image, after our likeness" (Genesis 1:26). Adam and Eve, according to Genesis 1 and 2, are created in a short space of time within the sixth day and in an immediately mature state. They are fully human, God's image bearers, body and soul, from the moment of receiving the breath of life.

Theistic evolutionists are all over the map on how human origins are to be reconciled to Genesis: Some say Adam had non-human hominid parents and evolved, after which God gave him a soul at some point of maturity, and then God created Eve from his rib in a special act of creation.[11] Others argue that Adam became human simply by virtue of God coming into a spiritual relationship with him, or that Adam became human by becoming religious. Yet others argue that Adam and Eve are just figures made up by Moses to represent a general transition of a large number of hominids into humans, or that perhaps Adam was the chief of a tribe where this took place.[12]

But all of this raises the question: if man evolved and became human through God imparting a spirit/soul or through a spiritual relationship, when does human life begin now? Conception? Later on? Adulthood? These are not hypothetical questions. Francis Collins, a leading theistic evolutionist, argues that embryonic stem cell research is acceptable because he does not believe embryos are humans. Only with the literal view of Adam and Eve's creation origin do we see an integrity of all of human life, from the very beginning.

Marriage and Unity of Race

The creation account of Adam and Eve is of pivotal importance in the cultural debate on marriage, gender, and sexual orientation. A plain reading of the text of Genesis 1 and 2 indicates that God created the first man and woman in His own image: Adam a male, Eve a female.[13] God created the man from dust and the woman from man's

---

11. A view held by Derek Kidner and Tim Keller.

12. Held by Peter Enns and John Collins, respectively.

13. The remarkable extent of the implication of maleness and femaleness in sex is only recently beginning to be explored as extending far beyond genitals and hormones: every cell in a male body is male, every cell in a female body is female, and this has ongoing implications for our whole person. See, for example, Matt Fearer, "From Liability to Viability: Genes on the Y Chromosome Prove Essential for Male Survival" in *The Whitehead Institute News*, April 23, 2014 (http://wi.mit.edu/news

rib, and brought them together in marriage. This created the reality of the male and female sex and the reality that man was created to be sexually oriented to the woman, and vice versa. Genesis provides the creative, normative, good pattern for sexual orientation in its expression within heterosexual marriage (Gen. 2:24–25). Marriage is also a means of fruitfulness—multiplication by procreation. Adam and Eve are the first parents of the entire human race (Acts 17:26).

While there is a place scripturally for celibacy (1 Corinthians 7), Scripture expressly rejects as sin a heterosexual orientation or relationship which rejects the boundaries of biblical marriage. Scripture also rejects a homosexual orientation or relationship as sin, noting that this also violates creation order intentionality by rejecting natural relations (Romans 1:26–27). According to biblical definition, homosexual orientation or relationship by its very essence rejects the boundaries of biblical marriage. Scripture also consistently indicates that gender is coherent with one's sex, though there is a range of scripturally legitimate expression of both masculinity and femininity. At the same time, biblical Christianity recognizes that the fall into sin was physical as well as spiritual. In the realm of human sexuality, these include intersex chromosomal and other disorders leading to physical anomalies. While some of these disorders are medically treatable and many still clearly present as ultimately either male or female, some are not easily treatable and remain part of the groaning of creation under the curse, waiting to find its healing in the resurrection and new creation.

In contrast to the literal reading of Genesis 1 and 2, non-literal views of human origins that adopt evolutionary biological models remove a significant scriptural warrant for the arguments given above. Most theistic evolutionary proponents argue that the violence we see today in the natural realm has always been. Bloodshed and death, at least in the animal realm, were part of God's very good creation prior to the fall into sin. If this is the case, where we see homosexual activity in the animal kingdom there is every reason to argue that this is also part of God's created order. Proponents of

/archive/2014/liability-viability-genes-y-chromosome-prove-essential-male-survival); Kalpit Shah, Charles E. McCormack, and Neil A. Bradbury, "Do you know the sex of your cells?" in *American Journal of Physiology—Cell Physiology*, January 2014, 306 (1) C3–C18.

evolutionary biological origins see a direct continuity of ancestral lineage between animal and human. As a result, according to the accepted canons of evolutionary theory, there is every reason to believe that homosexuality is an innate aspect of God's good creation. The same is true for polygamy.

Evolutionary biological models allow for a definition of humanity that includes variable degrees of evolutionary advancement between distinct races of humanity. This is true whether one holds to a model of monogenism or a dispersed polygenism. The effect of such an evolutionary model of human origins is found in the fact that even the taxonomy of many American government forms list "African-American" or "black" as a separate race from "Caucasian" or "white." This stands in contrast to those who hold to a literal Genesis on human origins: where there is only one race of humanity, all are Adam and Eve's children. The literal understanding of Genesis reveals the reality of a great diversity of ethnicities and cultures, but all peoples have an essential creational unity and equality. While this is broken through sin, restoration is found in the person and work of Christ, the second Adam.

God the Creator and the Goodness of His Creation

God is good, holy, gracious, omnipotent, and unchangingly faithful. All of God's attributes stand in perfect harmony with a literal understanding of our creation origins as very good. By contrast, theistic evolutionary views face a significant difficulty, as they must allow for suffering and death within the parameters of God's creating work and the pre-fall world. This raises some serious questions: How could it be very good of God to allow animals to suffer and die? Is it very good to allow the ancestors of humanity to suffer and die—all in a world where there has not been a fall into sin?

In the literal understanding of human origins, there is no sin, suffering, or death prior to the fall. God's creation is very good. Prior to Satan's entry, there is no evil or curse. The world prior to the fall into sin was marvelous compared to the way things are now—one that we look forward to with hope of restoration. There will again come a day when the lion and the lamb lie down together, when beauty, peace, and order are restored in every way. In the new creation there will be nothing that causes pain or destroys. By contrast, the philosophical and theological system of theistic evolution requires violence, suffering, and death before the fall. The necessary implication of animal and even human ancestry experiencing suffering and death prior to the fall must be very good. Not only does this conflict with Scripture's teaching, but also undermines God's character, His own perfect goodness as Creator and Redeemer.

In Adam's Fall We Sinned All?

The Christian doctrine of original sin is one of the renewed frontlines in the Genesis debate. While the literal Genesis understanding of human origins and the fall is seamlessly consistent with the doctrines of sin and salvation, problematic issues arise when we deviate from it. If Adam had ancestors and contemporaries, did they sin? Did they die? Scripture indicates that through Adam's sin death has come to all men: how is this a consequence of sin, if there was already death prior to the fall? Some proponents of new approaches to Genesis, like John Walton, posit that God gave such an Adam conditional immortality: Adam functioned as a savior figure, but failed. Others argue that God somehow imputed Adam's sin to his contemporaries and retroactively to his ancestors: they died in anticipation of his sin. As contemporary evangelical writers publish these views, we need to note that they are acting as though they are prophets bearing new revelations. Neither Scripture nor science teaches these things. No matter how they seek to stretch and adjust definitions to justify these "new revelations" needed to justify an evolutionary approach, they stand in blatant contradiction to Scripture's teaching that says sin came into the world through one man, Adam, and death through sin (Romans 5; 1 Corinthians 15).

Christ as Creator and Redeemer

Colossians 1:15–17 tells us that Christ "is the image of the invisible God, the firstborn of every creature: for by him were all things created, that are in heaven, and that are in earth, visible and invisible, whether they be thrones, or dominions, or principalities, or powers: all things were created by him, and for him: and he is before all things, and by him all things consist." Hebrews 1 reiterates this truth, stating that through the Son, God created the world; the Son upholds all things by the word of his power. Ephesians 3:9 says that

God created all things through Jesus Christ. If Christ is the One who created all things and life did not come into being through the mediation of a providentially guided evolutionary process, this gives us an expectation in harmony with both the curse and promise of Genesis 3:15. God's curse brings a supernatural, profound change to the created order: sin is rebellion and disobedience brings misery. Its end is death. The whole creation now groans with decay, disease, and disorder, while at the same time remaining sovereignly sustained, ordered, and governed by God. And yet there is the promise. The very Christ who was so intimately involved in forming the first man is the One who will come as redeemer. The Creator is the Redeemer. So Isaiah 35, where the eyes of the blind are opened and the ears of the deaf unstopped, is a glorious prophecy of the coming of the Creator-Redeemer. All of Scripture is congruent with the Christ who creates man and places him in the Garden. And in the New Testament we see Him literally, supernaturally fulfilling all the promises and prophecies, having taken to Himself the very nature that he so tenderly created; even taking our nature in its fallen condition, yet without sin.

The wonder is that the One who formed man from the dust, breathed into him the breath of life, and placed rebel Adam under the curse, places Himself under the curse and penalty as the second Adam. The supernatural glory of the resurrection and ascension vindicates, crowns, and seals Christ's work as Creator and Redeemer. The One who created all things gains victory over sin, death, and the grave, rising from the dead completely contrary to the fallen, cursed state of the natural order. He is the one Man, the beloved eternal Son, the Word made flesh, with whom the Father is well-pleased. And He is the first-fruits: the One who has begun the literal, spiritual, and physical work of re-creation in and through Himself.

Genesis 1 and 2 are about the triune God. They are about Jesus Christ. They are the beginning of the gospel. This is why again it is so crucial that we get Genesis right. If you hold to theistic evolution, then Jesus Christ, in His incarnation and earthly ministry, has not fully participated in our humanity. Why? Because He has entered human existence at its most advanced stage. He has not participated incarnate in the earlier stages of humanity; He has not participated incarnate in the animal stages of our origins. His identification with us is incomplete.

Conclusion

The differences between the literal Genesis understanding of our origins and non-literal, evolutionary models are vast. Where we fail to grasp this we are in danger of losing the Word, blinded to the reality of who we are and who God is. If we undermine Genesis and Adam, we undermine the gospel and Christ. Albert Mohler states,

> The implications for biblical authority are clear, as is the fact that if these arguments hold sway, we will have to come up with an entirely new story of the Gospel metanarrative and the Bible's storyline. The denial of the historical Adam and Eve as the first parents of all humanity and the solitary first human pair severs the link between Adam and Christ which is so crucial to the gospel. If we do not know how the story of the Gospel begins, then we do not know what that story means. Make no mistake: a false start to the story produces a false grasp of the Gospel.[14]

If we understand the breathtaking wonder of what God has said and done in Genesis and its inseparable part in the gospel, we will not trade our birthright for a pot of primordial soup: we will worship our Creator and Redeemer.

---

14. R. Albert Mohler, Jr., "Foreword" in *The Quest for the Historical Adam*, xii.

THE GLORIOUS PROPERTIES
OF GOD'S WORD

CHAPTER 4

The Clarity of Scripture

Deuteronomy 30:11–14

Jack Schoeman

In his book *Taking God at His Word,* Kevin DeYoung recalls a time when he—along with several others—was invited to speak at a conference on the emergent church. Following a panel discussion on the subject, he was approached by a "furious" man. Throughout his speech, DeYoung had tried to prove, using Scripture, that certain teachings of the emergent church are not scriptural. This man wanted to know where DeYoung got the gall to claim that he knew what Scripture teaches. But every time DeYoung referred to a verse or passage of Scripture, the man simply said, "Well, that's just your interpretation." It soon became apparent that the discussion was not going anywhere because the two men had very different views of the doctrine of the clarity (or, to use the older term, "perspicuity") of Scripture.[1]

In so many ways, this story illustrates the confusion that exists within the church today on this vitally important subject. There are in the church today more and more voices that claim we cannot know for sure what the Bible says about almost anything. The Bible, they assert, is simply not clear—or at least not as clear as some Christians claim.[2]

Needless to say, much is at stake in this argument. First, the very authority of Scripture is at stake. If Scripture is not clear, then it is not authoritative. In this case, what Scripture says would not matter.

The accessibility of Scripture is also at stake. If Scripture is not clear, then why read it? Why study it? Why even preach from it?

---

1. Kevin DeYoung, *Taking God at His Word* (Wheaton, Ill.: Crossway, 2014), 57–58.
2. See, for example, Christian Smith's *The Bible Made Impossible* (Grand Rapids: Brazos Press, 2012).

Third, the applicability of Scripture is at stake. If Scripture is not clear, then why should we do what it says? Why should we repent? Why should we believe? Why should we live a holy life? And what does it matter what Scripture says—or seems to say—about homosexuality, abortion, euthanasia, and other moral issues? If Scripture is not clear, then it is irrelevant.

And finally, the doctrine of God is at stake. If Scripture is not clear, what does this say about God? Are we now to say that God is not capable of communicating His own thoughts clearly? R. C. Sproul writes, "What kind of God would reveal His love and redemption in terms so technical and concepts so profound that only an elite corps of professional scholars could understand them?"[3] To say that He does amounts to a denial of the very character of God.

Attacks on the clarity of Scripture, however, are not new. In fact, they can be traced back to the early sixteenth century to a debate between the great German Reformer Martin Luther and the great humanist scholar Desiderius Erasmus. In 1524, Erasmus published his most famous work, *De Libero Arbitrio* ("On Free Will"). In this book, Erasmus defended the Roman Catholic doctrine of the free will of man, against Luther, who denied it. What touched off the debate about the clarity of Scripture is what Erasmus wrote in the preface to his book. There Erasmus chided Luther for the way in which he engaged in theological discourse, particularly his frequent and confident appeals to Scripture. To Erasmus, no one could claim to know what Scripture taught on every point. Did the apostle Paul not exclaim, "O the depth of the riches both of the wisdom and knowledge of God! How unsearchable are his judgments, and his ways past finding out" (Rom. 11:33)? And did Isaiah not ask, "Who hath directed the Spirit of the LORD, or being his counsellor hath taught him" (Isa. 40:13)? According to Erasmus, if the judgments of God are indeed "unsearchable" and His ways "past finding out," then no one can know exactly what Scripture teaches about anything. For Luther to claim that he did was, to Erasmus, the height of arrogance and presumption, meaning that Luther could not be a true scholar of the Word.

Sixteen months later, Luther responded to Erasmus with the publication of what was arguably his greatest work, *De Servo Arbitrio*

---

3. R. C. Sproul, *Knowing Scripture* (Downers Grove, Ill.: InterVarsity Press, 1977), 16.

(*The Bondage of the Will*). In this book, Luther not only defended his view that fallen man has no free will, but he also responded to Erasmus's critique of his view of Scripture. Luther's response to Erasmus can be summarized in the following seven statements:

1. Nothing in Scripture is obscure.

2. Anything that seems to be obscure is so because of the ignorance of man, not the obscurity of Scripture.

3. Some texts are obscure because the reader does not understand key words and grammar.

4. Satan also tries to blind human eyes to the meaning of Scripture.

5. If a scriptural topic seems to be obscure in one place, it will be clear in other places.

6. Whatever is not clear in Scripture is not to be ascribed to Scripture itself, but rather to our own depravity.

7. There are two kinds of clarity in Scripture: one external, the other internal. External clarity extends to the whole world, not just Christians. Internal clarity comes from the Holy Spirit.[4]

Luther's response to Erasmus, though seminal, was not the final word on this subject. Some 125 years later, the Westminster divines dedicated an article to this subject in the *Westminster Confession of Faith* (1.7), where they declared that "all things in Scripture are not alike plain in themselves, nor alike clear unto all: yet those things which are necessary to be known, believed, and observed for salvation are so clearly propounded, and opened in some place of Scripture or other, that not only the learned, but the unlearned, in a due use of the ordinary means, may attain unto a sufficient understanding of them." Here it is stated that Scripture is so clear that even the "unlearned" can understand its basic meaning and message.

In asserting this truth, however, it is worth noting that the Westminster divines felt the need to qualify it in several important ways. They admitted, for example, that some portions of Scripture are clearer than others; not every passage has an obvious meaning. As

---

4. Peter A. Lillback and Richard B. Gaffin Jr., ed., *Thy Word is Still Truth* (Phillipsburg, N.J.: P&R, 2013), 7–9.

evidence of this they cited 2 Peter 3:16 in which the apostle Peter (who was inspired by and filled with the Holy Spirit) writes that some of the writings of Paul contain matters that are "hard to be understood." They also admitted that not every doctrine is clear in every passage, although they are all made clear in other passages. They further admitted that Scripture is not so clear that it can be readily understood without the use of "means" (e.g., sermons, commentaries, exegetical aids, etc.). But they rightly insisted that, with respect to its main meaning and message, Scripture is clear. As James Callahan observes, the doctrine of the clarity of Scripture teaches that "Scripture is clear about what it is about."[5]

This is clearly scriptural. The fact is, Scripture everywhere assumes—and even at times asserts—its own clarity. The classic text in this regard is Deuteronomy 30:11–14, in which Moses writes, "For this commandment which I command thee this day, it is not hidden from thee, neither is it far off. It is not in heaven, that thou shouldest say, Who shall go up for us to heaven, and bring it unto us, that we may hear it, and do it? Neither is it beyond the sea, that thou shouldest say, Who shall go over the sea for us, and bring it unto us, that we may hear it, and do it? But the word is very nigh unto thee, in thy mouth, and in thy heart, that thou mayest do it." Moses here declares that the Word of God is near, not far. The idea is that the Word of God is not beyond us. Rather, it can be understood by everyone to the point that we are able to "do" it (and even be punished if we do not).

This same sentiment is echoed in many of the psalms. For example, in Psalm 19:7 David declares, "The law of the LORD is perfect, converting the soul: the testimony of the LORD is sure, making wise the simple." If the Word of the Lord were not clear, how could it convert the soul? How could it make the simple wise?

Similarly, in Psalm 119:105 the psalmist compares the Word of God to a lamp: "Thy word is a lamp unto my feet, and a light unto my path." If the Word of God were not clear, how could it function to guide our path as does a lamp?

Verses in the New Testament reflect a similar emphasis. Whenever Jesus was asked for his opinion on a matter of doctrine or

---

5. James Patrick Callahan, "*Claritas Scripturae*: The Role of Perspicuity in Protestant Hermeneutics," *Journal of the Evangelical Theological Society* 39, no. 3 (Sept. 1996):353–72.

whenever He responded to an accusation by the religious leaders of the Jews, He often responded by asking those accusers if they had read certain verses of the Old Testament.

In doing so Jesus did two things: First, He affirmed that the Old Testament is authoritative. Second, He affirmed that the Old Testament is clear and understandable. This is confirmed by the fact that, in most cases, whenever Jesus quoted the Old Testament, He did so without further commentary; He simply let the words stand on their own.

We see this same pattern in the epistles. Whenever the apostles quote the Old Testament to establish a doctrinal teaching (which they do very often—more than three hundred times), they invariably assume that the Old Testament is authoritative and clear.

What is more, we would do well to remember that most of the New Testament epistles are written not to "experts" but to congregations, which implies that the apostles expected everyone in the church (Jews, Gentiles, and even children) to understand, at least to some degree, what they wrote.

Although this may seem obvious to many, it is not to many others. In his book *A Clear and Present Word*, Mark D. Thompson mentions five objections to the doctrine of the clarity of Scripture. Some of these objections are quite old; others are new, but are simply reformulations of old objections.

1. The doctrine fails to account for the transcendent mystery that is the subject of Scripture, namely, God Himself. According to this view, God is so transcendent we cannot adequately describe Him or His will in words. We cannot put God in a box, nor can we reduce His will for man to a series of theological propositions. To do so is proud and presumptuous.

2. The doctrine fails to acknowledge the God-given role of the church as the interpreter of Scripture. This was the common objection of the Roman Catholic Church during the time of the Reformation. In their view, Scripture in and of itself is not clear. It must be interpreted, and this task belongs to the church alone. The Bible means what the church says it means.

3. The doctrine fails to take seriously the nature of the words of Scripture. According to this view, because Scripture is written in human words, we are prone to misunderstand and misinterpret it.

To claim that Scripture is clear, therefore, is to expect more of its words than they are able to deliver.

4. The doctrine fails in practice given the reality of diverse interpretations. In other words, if Scripture is so clear, why are there so many differing interpretations and denominations?

5. The doctrine fails by its own criterion since Scripture confesses its own obscurity. This is why David in Psalm 119 prays to God to open his eyes so that he might behold wondrous things out of His law. This is why the two men on the way to Emmaus and the Ethiopian eunuch needed the help of others in order to understand Scripture. None of this would be necessary if Scripture were clear.[6]

Suffice it to say that not a single one of these objections is compelling enough to cause us to deny the clarity of Scripture. That is mainly due to the fact that many of these objections are levelled against claims that the historic doctrine of the clarity of Scripture simply does not make. For example, the doctrine of the clarity of Scripture—as historically defined—does not claim and has never claimed that all of Scripture is clear to everyone. Nor does it claim that it does not contain certain passages that are difficult to interpret. Nor does it claim that Scripture is so clear that external aids are not necessary. In fact, it claims the exact opposite. All it claims is that whatever is necessary to know and to be believed for salvation is clearly revealed—nothing more and nothing less.

There is, however, one objection to the doctrine of the clarity of Scripture that merits some discussion. It is the fourth objection mentioned above: if Scripture is clear, why are there so many different interpretations of it and so many different denominations?

This objection has been given new life recently in the publication of Christian Smith's book, *The Bible Made Impossible*. Smith's basic thesis is that "the biblicism that pervades much of American evangelicalism is untenable and needs to be abandoned in favour of a better approach to Christian truth and authority." By "biblicism" Smith means "a particular theory about and style of using the Bible that is defined by a constellation of related assumptions and beliefs about the Bible's nature, purpose, and function."[7] At the heart of

6. Mark D. Thompson, *A Clear and Present Word: The Clarity of Scripture* (Downers Grove, Ill.: InterVarsity Press, 2006), 19–30.

7. Smith, *The Bible Made Impossible*, 3–4.

Smith's critique of "biblicism" is what he refers to as the problem of "pervasive interpretive pluralism," that is, many Bible-believing Christians hold to vastly differing views on several significant theological matters such as how the church should be governed, whether man has free will, how Christians should observe the Lord's Day, the morality of slavery, the role of women in the church, whether Christians may ever go to war, the place of charismatic gifts in the church today, how Christians should worship God, etc. According to Smith, the fact that many Christians disagree about these and other matters means that the Bible is not clear.

Much already has been said about Smith's book. Although there are, sadly, many differences of interpretation within the Christian church—some of which admittedly touch on weighty matters—most of these differences do not impact the cardinal doctrines of the Christian faith. Most Christian denominations believe and uphold the articles of the Christian faith contained in the so-called ecumenical creeds: the Apostles' Creed, the Nicene Creed, and the Athanasian Creed. This is true even of Roman Catholics. This remarkable degree of unanimity only serves to reinforce the argument that Scripture is clear in terms of its basic message.

In addition, consider these two points. First, we must never underestimate the noetic effects of the fall of man into sin. The word "noetic" is derived from the Greek word "nous" meaning "mind." When we refer to the noetic effects of the fall into sin we are referring to the effect of the fall on man's understanding and his ability to comprehend spiritual things. Since the fall, man does not rightly understand spiritual things. The apostle Paul writes, "But the natural man receiveth not the things of the Spirit of God: for they are foolishness unto him: neither can he know them, because they are spiritually discerned" (1 Cor. 2:14). The only way man can understand the things of the Spirit of God is when he is enlightened by the Spirit of God. Therefore, if there are differences—or even errors—among sincere, Bible-believing Christians, at least part of the reason for this lies not in the fact that Scripture is not clear, but in the fact that man's mind is not what it used to be. The truth is, apart from the enlightening work of the Holy Spirit, man by nature is utterly incapable of grasping the full depth and breadth of spiritual truth.

Second, we must remember that in some cases God deliberately prevents understanding. This is made clear in Isaiah 6:9–10 in which, after commissioning Isaiah to go and preach His word, God instructs him on what to say: "Hear ye indeed, but understand not; and see ye indeed, but perceive not. Make the heart of this people fat, and make their ears heavy, and shut their eyes; lest they see with their eyes, and hear with their ears, and understand with their heart, and convert, and be healed." Interestingly, Jesus quotes these verses in Matthew 13:14–15 to explain why He speaks to the people in parables: "And in [those who do not understand the meaning of these parables] is fulfilled the prophecy of Esaias, which saith, By hearing ye shall hear, and shall not understand; and seeing ye shall see, and shall not perceive: for this people's heart is waxed gross, and their ears are dull of hearing, and their eyes they have closed; lest at any time they should see with their eyes and hear with their ears, and should understand with their heart, and should be converted, and I should heal them."

Jesus here declares that the twofold reason he speaks to the people in parables is to enlighten those who are His disciples and to keep in the dark those who are not. To quote John Frame, "the clarity of the Word…is selective. It is for some, not all. It is for those with whom God intends to fully communicate."[8] Why God chooses to reveal His truth to some and not to others is not known. All we can say is that God is sovereign. He is the potter and we are merely lumps of clay.

The point is, no matter how many differing interpretations of Scripture there are or may be in the future, the fault for this does not lie with the Word of God. The Word of God is clear.

So what does this mean for you and me? Allow me to make four brief applications.

1. Since the Word of God is clear, we should proclaim it with confidence—both the very clear and the not so clear parts. This point is especially applicable to preachers. It is tempting as a preacher to avoid those passages that are controversial or difficult to interpret. We need to avoid this temptation. If all of Scripture is "given by inspiration of God, and is profitable for doctrine, for reproof, for correction, for instruction in righteousness" (2 Tim. 3:16), then all of it

---

8. John Frame, *The Doctrine of the Word of God* (Phillipsburg, N.J.: P&R, 2010), 205.

should be preached. This may require extra study. It may require much wrestling before the Lord, but it must be done by ministers of the gospel.

2. Since the Word of God is clear, we should read, study, and meditate on it daily—personally, with our families, and in group settings—with the prayer that the Holy Spirit may open our eyes to understand and apply it in the right way. Like the psalmist, we should be a people who "meditate" on the law of God "day and night," trusting that what we are reading is the Word of God and that God has written it in such a way that we can understand it and apply it to our lives.

3. Since the Word of God is clear, we should believe what it teaches. It is to be lamented that a growing number of people in church today seem to feel they have the right to question the teaching of Scripture on almost everything. There are questions being raised about whether God created the world in six literal, 24-hour days, whether women should serve in the offices of the church, whether the Bible condemns homosexuality, whether marriage is between a man and woman, and a whole host of issues. At root, all such questions have their origin in the question that Satan asked Eve in the Garden: "Yea, hath God said?" (Gen. 3:1). Our calling as Christians is not to reconcile the Word of God with science and sociology and psychology and all other fields of human inquiry. Our calling as Christians is to believe what God says. Anything more than this stems from unbelief.

4. Since the Word of God is clear, we should do what it says. That means different things to different people depending on their spiritual condition before God. If you are not saved, the Bible tells you to repent and believe on the Lord Jesus Christ lest you perish in your sins. If you are saved, the Bible tells you to put sin to death in your life and live for the glory of God. Are you doing that? Are you obeying the invitations and commands of Scripture? Or are you seeking to evade them by coming up with all kinds of excuses and setting forth all kinds of conditions? Let us never seek to hide behind alleged obscurities in Scripture. With respect to its main message, Scripture is abundantly clear. The question is, are we doing what Scripture teaches and commands?

The great English Reformer William Tyndale suffered greatly for his efforts to translate the Bible into the common language of the people. On one occasion, while disputing with a supposedly "learned" man, he said, "If God spare my life [before] many years I will cause a boy that driveth the plough to know more of Scripture than thou dost." Tyndale believed in the clarity of Scripture. And he paid for it with his life. He died by strangulation and his corpse was burned in the city square.

Fittingly, just before his death he cried out for all to hear, "Lord, open the King of England's eyes!" This is a prayer we need to pray still today, for ourselves, for the church, and for the world. The Word of God is clear. May the Lord open our eyes to see and to believe all that it contains.

CHAPTER 5

The Sufficiency of Scripture

Luke 16:31

Geoff Thomas

Our Lord Jesus Christ tells of two men, a rich man who rejected God and a beggar whose trust was in the Lord. Both of them died, and the beggar went to heaven while the rich man went to hell (Luke 16:19–31). One of the reasons He tells this story is that we may know something of what lies after death. Many will enjoy the pleasures of heaven but others will suffer the horrors of hell. That is the conscious experience of all who die. We all live in a room and there are two exits. On the one *Heaven* is written and on the other *Hell*. There is no other door. There is no purgatory; there is no second chance after death; there is no soul sleep; there is no limbo. There is no such thing as the annihilation of the soul, but there is, after death, judgment followed by heaven or hell. The Son of God is emphasizing here that souls do not die as bodies do, but after death the souls of men and women live on and are immediately, consciously, and intelligently aware of the love or wrath of God.

This rich man who was suffering the torments of hell holds a conversation with Abraham. It is with this patriarch in particular because Abraham is the father of all who believe. God once spoke to Abraham and made great promises to him. God pointed out the stars and said that He would so bless Abraham that his progeny would become as numerous as the lights of heaven. He would give Abraham a child in his old age and through this child all the nations of the earth would be blessed, because one day in the line of Abraham's own son a child would be born who would be the Savior of the world.

Abraham responded by believing all that God said. He left his house in Ur and set out with his family to this unknown place that God said He was preparing for him. In such trust Abraham became a real model for all who similarly hear the Word of God, believe, and are justified. All men have sinned and deserve the judgment of God forever, but the Lord has provided redemption through the Messiah, Jesus Christ. Through Him believers in all the nations of the earth are blessed with the gospel of salvation when they entrust themselves to the Son of God alone. All of these believers, then, come into the blessing of glory after death. Jesus says, "In my Father's house are many mansions: if it were not so, I would have told you. I go to prepare a place for you" (John 14:2). He says to the dying thief who believed in Him, "Today shalt thou be with me in Paradise" (Luke 23:43b). One day He will say to those on His right hand: "Come, ye blessed of my Father, inherit the kingdom prepared for you from the foundation of the world" (Matt. 25:34). The beggar in Luke 16 is one of those who trusted in the Son of God.

The same Savior who speaks of heaven also speaks in unambiguous language warning the world of the awful truth of the place of woe, of the worm that does not die, the flames that are not quenched, the wailing and gnashing of teeth, the outer darkness, the everlasting fire prepared for the devil and his angels. The Lord Jesus taught that hell is real, is ruled by God, and is characterized by rejection and pain. He said more about it than anyone else in the Bible. If we are serious in our understanding of the Man who preached the Sermon on the Mount; whom the waves and winds obeyed when He addressed them; who healed the incurable elderly, who in the last stages of his illness came to Jesus of Nazareth for life; who even raised the dead and who was Himself resurrected—then we must take whatever He says with the utmost gravity. We must reckon with the fact that this Man of integrity, patience, and love says plainly that some people will spend eternity in hell. Although He says that this present life is important, it is not all-important.

So the Lord Jesus tells this parable. The three main characters in the parable before us are Abraham, the rich man, and Lazarus. Abraham is the spokesman for God. The rich man represents every unrepentant man. The name Lazarus means "God helps" and so the poor beggar signifies those who have received the saving help of God. The parable has this great theme of "being too late." The rich man pays attention to Lazarus too late; he sees the unbridgeable chasm too late; he worries about his brothers too late; and he heeds the law and the prophets too late.

The First Conversation

The first conversation of the man in hell concerns a request that he might be relieved of his unbearable torment. But Abraham tells him that this is impossible, in effect saying, "All your lifetime you received good things; you were reminded of the certainty of death and judgment; you were warned to flee from the wrath to come; you were told of the mercy and long-suffering of the grace of God; you were told to seek that mercy and find peace through the gospel." But after death it is too late. Mercy is unattainable; death fixes the destinies of men and women forever, and in hell he is experiencing the justice of God and he will do so forever. Some might think that is unfair, but only God is an adequate judge of what sinners deserve.

The rich man's condition, then, cannot change; there is no hope. There is a great gulf between him and those who are in the presence of Abraham, because those who are there did entrust themselves, their lives and every detail of every day, into the hands of a faithful Savior. Those who are in hell cannot cross over that impassable gulf. There is no possibility of a change from the one estate to another. Abraham tells the rich man this awful fact.

The Second Conversation

The second request of the man in hell deals with his five brethren. These brothers are still in the world, so the man in the pit devises a scheme by which they would not join him there, because their presence, no doubt, would make his hell five times worse. So he devises a plan of evangelism, which many human beings do. He imagines a way of delivering his siblings from the place of woe. The five brothers all know the beggar who lived his life at the gate of their rich brother's house. He was always there, and they all knew that he had died. So the rich man says, in essence, to Abraham, "Send that man, Lazarus, from your side back to my brothers to show himself to them as one raised from the dead. The result of that will be that they will all become believers, especially when he tells them about hell. If a man should be raised from the dead and should tell them what is happening to me, they will change. They will no longer curl their lip and say, 'Nobody's ever come back,' but they will believe in God and escape hell."

This is the wisdom of a man in hell. This is his proposal. From this request arises a discussion between Abraham and the rich man. Abraham argues one side and the man in hell argues the other side. Abraham defends the position of those who believe in God through the Lord Jesus Christ, and the man in hell defends the position of those who use human reason and never trust the Savior in this world nor the next. This argument is going on still, and it is important for us to see what this argument consists of and the difference between the two approaches.

On one side there is Abraham and all who believe as he did. One thing is true of every one of them, and that is that they are satisfied with the Bible. Theologically we would say that they hold to the sufficiency of Scripture to save any person from hell. In verse 29 Abraham says, "They have Moses and the prophets; let them hear them." Moses wrote the first five books of the Bible. There is Genesis which tells us that God is a personal God and an almighty Lord, how He made the world, and why the world is in its current state. It speaks of the great answer to man's rebellion in the Christ who one day will come and bruise the serpent's head. Then in Exodus we are told of the Passover, of those for whom a lamb had died substitutionally, and how the angel of death had passed over all of them. Because of the lamb that had shed its blood they were forgiven. Leviticus 17:11 tells us that "it is the blood that maketh an atonement for the soul," and Hebrews 9:22 says that "without shedding of blood there is no remission" of sins. These verses point to the sacrifices of redemption instituted by a loving God. Numbers 21 tells us of the brazen serpent lifted up in the wilderness and if men obediently look on who and what that represents they will have life. The book of Deuteronomy tells us of the covenant relationship between God and his people, the great Jehovah, the I Am, pledging Himself to be their God and Savior forever and ever.

"They have Moses," Abraham says. In addition, the rich man's brothers had all the rest of the Old Testament written by the prophets who together speak of the Lord Jesus Christ. He is there in it all. So Abraham says, "Let them listen to them." How much more should we today listen to those who were eyewitnesses of Jesus's majesty, who were with Him in the upper room, who heard His command, "Peace, be still" (Mark 4:39), and who saw the waves obey him, and who helped unloose risen Lazarus from his grave clothes. Should we not listen to them who by the Holy Spirit were led into all truth in what they wrote? Do you see Abraham's argument? Scripture is enough to bring a man to faith in Jesus Christ. Scripture itself is more than sufficient to save a man from hell.

Then Abraham adds in words to this effect in verse 31: "If they do not listen to the Bible, nothing else will convince them; nothing else will do any good, not even the specter of a resurrection before their very eyes." So the question is, do you agree with Abraham? On the one side of the debate (v. 27) the man in hell is saying that it seems a great idea to him to send a man back from the grave to the world of the living to warn others. But Abraham says, "They have Scripture, let them hear it." "No," the rich man responds, "the Bible is not enough; it is not sufficient." He has no confidence in the Word of God. He is saying, "They need something more than the Bible if they are going to be saved from hell." This man thinks that the Bible is an ineffective book, that you cannot expect anyone to get serious about eternal life and flee from the wrath to come simply by reading the Bible, or by hearing sermons from Scripture.

Now, it is very interesting that the man in hell addresses Abraham respectfully, calling him "Father Abraham," and that the patriarch acknowledges that and responds to him with the word "son." In other words, this man is a fellow Jew, a member of the Old Testament covenant people. He has been circumcised; ethnically and outwardly he is a son of Abraham. The Lord Jesus in Luke 16 is speaking to fellow countrymen. He is addressing the Pharisees who are sneering at Him ("And the Pharisees also, who were covetous, heard all these things: and they derided him," verse 14). They cannot imagine that they themselves are in any danger of hell. Even when they see Lazarus raised from the dead they continue their plotting to kill the Lord Jesus Christ.

This rich man, then, grew up in the synagogue, memorizing Scripture, hearing it week by week. But he never obeyed it, nor did he love it; instead he found it boring. He never dreamed for a moment that he would end up in hell. He never thought that one day there would be a great chasm fixed between himself and Abraham. There are many like him who hear the Word of God preached with the Holy Ghost sent down from heaven. Judas heard it; Ananias heard it; Sapphira heard it; Demas heard it; the Judaisers heard it—but all were lost.

Now, you see what the rich man is essentially saying from hell: "If Scripture is the only thing that you are going to give my brothers, well...I had it, and what good did it do me? It did not change me." In fact, he is saying in hell, deep within his heart: "It is perfectly understandable that I didn't believe and that they don't believe; all we had was the Bible. I know my brothers; I am aware how they live; I know where they are going. The Bible is not going to touch them. Those kinds of men need something more." In effect, he is saying: "It is excusable; if only I had seen a miracle that thrilled me, I would have believed. If a man had been raised from the dead and spoken to me, then I would have paid attention. If I could have gone to a meeting where amazing things happened, it would have been different. But all I had was the Bible. The Bible!" That is what many people say still. "You don't expect the world to be attracted by the Bible, by the preaching of Scripture, by texts outside chapels, by tracts with Scripture on them, by memorizing the Bible, by lessons from the Bible to children in Sunday School, by camps where young people are taught the Bible, or by conferences where the Bible is proclaimed. You don't expect people to be attracted by that. We need concerts! We need drama! We need costumes! We need bands! We need choreography! Bring in the drums and the synthesizers. Send for the clowns! Then the people will come. We need superstars and celebrities to give us their testimonies, not just the Bible alone!" But, you see, Abraham is unyielding. "The Bible is sufficient," he says.

Now there are many religious people who argue like that man from hell. The Roman Catholic Church says that the Bible is not enough, we must have Sacred Tradition too. The Quakers say that the Bible is not enough, but there must be an inner voice in the congregation. Modernists say Scripture itself is not enough; it must be interpreted by the assured results of modern criticism. They say that we must go back to sources *behind* our present gospel narratives to find the *authentic* sayings of Jesus. Cults say the Bible is not enough and that men must obey another book—the Book of Mormon, or *Science and Health With Key to the Scriptures* by Mary Baker Eddy, or the Watchtower's productions of the Jehovah's Witnesses. Many Charismatics say that the Bible is not enough, that it needs to be authenticated by miracles and signs. All such people are saying that the Bible is not good enough. They say: "It's a good start, but it needs a bit of help from us."

Some even dare to say that when the apostle Paul was preaching in Athens he slipped up and as a result few were converted. Paul used wrong methods; all he did was preach the Word of God sensitively to the philosophers who were gathered there on Mars Hill and only a few were converted. So Paul went to Corinth and he drastically changed his methods and performed miracles and many were converted. But the conversion of one of the members of the Greek supreme court named Dionysius, and a woman named Damaris, as well as a number of other people converted (Acts 17:34) would be considered by us to be very encouraging for the first meeting in a community that had never heard the gospel before. But people are taught that this is not "power evangelism," that unless we can do miracles, there will be no converts.

"No, Father Abraham," says the man in hell, "not the Bible alone—the Bible plus." The Bible plus informal entertainment. The Bible plus background music. You choose the plus; you enthuse about it; you give lectures about it and write books about it; you can grow rich on it: "How I found the plus that helps the rather inadequate Bible." You can hold summer schools and conferences and tell the world the method that you discovered of compensating for the failure of Scripture, just like this man in hell who had no love for God who thought of a way that could make up for the inadequacies of the Bible.

Now remember Abraham was in heaven before Moses wrote the first five books of the Bible. He had a unique perspective on the books of Moses and the prophets. Abraham was there in the presence of God when the Lord gave the Word to Moses and to the prophets. He was listening to the Lord on those occasions when God commanded the Holy Spirit, the Spirit of illumination, "Go to Moses, Samuel, David, Solomon, Elijah, Isaiah, Jeremiah, and Ezekiel and assist them to understand my word, proclaim it, and write Scripture." Abraham heard God speak, and he knew the source and power of that voice which had come from the throne of the universe. From the lips of the living God had come those words. Abraham knew and loved them; they were Spirit and life. They were powerful words, as effectual as when God had said, "Let there be light," and there was light

(Gen. 1:3). The Almighty has broken the silence of the heavens. God has spoken to sinners. He has opened His heart and revealed His inmost being. He is there and He is not silent. We have His Word. "God, who at sundry times and in divers manners spake in time past unto the fathers by the prophets, hath in these last days spoken unto us by his Son, whom he hath appointed heir of all things, by whom also he made the worlds" (Heb. 1:1–2). He is a speaking God, but now in these last days He has spoken through His Son, the Lord from heaven, the speaking Savior, the Prophet, God's final Word. The Lord Christ has said that no one knows the Father save the Son, He alone having that infinite acquaintance. There is the immensity of the Almighty and only the Son knows Him comprehensively. When at the end of Jesus's mortal life He was praying, He thanked the Father for all the help that He has had to discharge the commission which the Father had given Him. He had omitted nothing, and when Jesus sends His apostles into the world He gives them the Holy Spirit to lead them into all truth, and they also omit nothing. Everything has been provided for all that is needed for the two thousand years of the church's history. When Paul acknowledges himself as an apostle he says, "And last of all he was seen of me also" (1 Cor. 15:8). In other words, Paul is the last apostle. No more apostles are needed. No house needs more than one satisfactory foundation.

We have Moses, we have the prophets, we have the Gospels, and we have the epistles. We have them all in our own language. We may hold them in our hands and we can read them. Once, when John Jewel, one of the great English Reformers who became the Bishop of Salisbury, was preaching on Scripture, he ended by rousing his congregation: "Are you a father? Have you children? Read the Scriptures. Are you a king? Read the Scriptures. Are you a minister? Read the Scriptures. Has God blessed you with wealth? Read the Scriptures. Are you a usurer? Read the Scriptures. Are you a fornicator? Read the Scriptures. Are you in adversity? Read the Scriptures. Are you a sinner? Have you offended God? Read the Scriptures. Do you despair of the mercy of God? Read the Scriptures. Are you going out of this life? Read the Scriptures."[1]

---

1. Cf. John Jewel, *The Works of John Jewel* (Cambridge: The University Press, 1845), 4:1175–77.

Abraham is saying words to this effect: "Do you want your brothers to see a miracle? Your brothers have got a miracle; they hear at every visit to the synagogue Moses and the prophets. They may purchase for themselves Moses and the prophets. They may read and memorize Moses and the prophets." We who live twenty centuries later have more, having the Gospels, the Acts, the letters, and the book of Revelation. These new covenant writings are the miracle which leads the church into the new millennium. When I take this Bible in my hand, I am holding a mighty work of God. I have something absolutely unique. Here is something miraculous in its independence of thought, in the comprehensiveness of its theme, its utter and invincible confidence that it is the most relevant Word to my own life and to that of every man. Sometimes in moments of doubt our minds must rest simply in this: we have the Bible. We have this great intrusion from heaven, this book that comes from another world in which men may hear the unique utterances of the Son of God. We may have read much of human literature at its best but we find here in this book something that is discontinuous with everything else. Here is a book which is absolutely unique. The Bible is a word from God that knows us, that describes us, that searches us, that finds us. Scripture speaks to man's deepest needs. Here are words that contain concepts of unsurpassable grandeur, words that are invincible in their sheer originality.

Every Sunday when gospel churches meet they do so around this miracle of the altogether sufficient Bible. Every single service has at its center this miracle, and not just on those red-letter Sundays when everything is just right. Not merely when the Holy Spirit comes, convicts, and moves, but every time we are gathered in the name of the Lord Jesus Christ and this book is in the center of our gathering... then we are meeting in the presence of a miracle. Do you say you want a miracle and then you will believe? Well, here is a miracle! Abraham says "No!" to signs and wonders as the means of saving sinners today, because here is the Bible and it is a miracle in itself. "So then faith cometh by hearing, and hearing by the word of God" (Rom. 10:17). Abraham knew that this was the divine method.

So then, you must go to a church where there is a man sent to preach the Word of Christ. That has been and always will be the means of saving anyone. Not since the apostolic age has a single person come to faith in Christ through seeing someone raised from the dead, but millions have become believers through hearing the Word. Abraham knew that all the children that were now there with him in the presence of God had been saved through the Bible, and that the millions more who would join him there would get to heaven in the same way. It was Scripture which made them all "wise unto salvation through faith which is in Christ Jesus" (2 Tim. 3:15). God in mercy has said: "I have as many people coming into the kingdom as the sands on the seashore; they are all going to share heaven with me. They are corrupted rebels. They provoke me dreadfully, but I will forgive their sins, and I will do this for all who have believed in Jesus Christ. And this will be the way—by bringing my Word to them. I will send them a Christian neighbor; I will put them in a university and there they will meet witnessing students. I will work through a member of their family, or through the woman who works in that office with them, and I will bring them all to a congregation where they will hear the Word of God preached. That is the way I will rescue them from hell. They do not have to be scholars to understand Scripture, but I will open their understanding to know the way of salvation through faith in Christ which is found so plainly in the Bible." Psalm 19:7 says that "the testimony of the LORD is sure, making wise the simple." Ordinary folk can read or hear this message of the gospel and understand it. It tells us that we deserve eternal hell because we are sinners, but Jesus, because he loved us, died for us that we might be saved. We have that message. If men will not listen to it, they will not be convinced even if God should change teeth fillings from amalgam to gold.

Scripture is sufficient to make the man of God perfect. How far can Scripture take you? It can take you to total maturity, that is to be "thoroughly furnished unto all good works" (2 Tim. 3:17). What lies before us? What duties, challenges, and sacrifices will we be called upon to meet? The Bible will completely equip us for them. How may we grow and put away childish things? How can we become mature men and women? How will we become wise? How may we become conformed to the image of Christ? Through following the Bible—that is the divine way. Scripture sanctifies and perfects what is imperfect. It thoroughly enables us for the challenge of every good work in whatever God asks us to do. Every mountain God asks us to climb, every burden God asks us to bear, every service God asks us to give, every pressure God asks us to endure, every sacrifice God asks us to make...Scripture can enable us to do it all by comprehensively preparing us for every single good work. It tells us how to do it, tells us why we should do it, gives us strength for the task, and also warns us how not to do it. Scripture will complete that good work which God has begun in us. It is a supernatural blessing to have the Bible.

Our Lord Jesus Christ ends the Sermon on the Mount by speaking about a wise man who built his house upon a rock; the storms, winds, and floods came, and the house still stood. That man was building his life on the teaching of the Lord Jesus and he stood. Christ was looking forward down the centuries, even looking into the hideous twentieth century in which we have lived for so long. Christ knew all the storms that would be hurled at little Christian boys and girls: the gales of scientific pretension, of philosophy and humanism, of materialism and fleshliness. Yet every young Christian who stands on the teaching of Jesus will survive any storm. The Savior is absolutely confident about it.

The professing church is in a hopeless, demoralized state should its members begin to believe that the Bible is insufficient for the task before us. The Roman Catholic Church, the Quakers, the Modernists, the cults, and the Charismatics are all looking for some additional signs and voices. None of them is in a healthy state; none of them is convinced about the sufficiency of divine truth. The issue confronting the Christian is, are you contented with the Bible or not?

One man was presented with what Scripture was saying, verse after verse being quoted to him. Finally, he said in his opposition to those truths, "Let's close the book and listen to the Spirit." Now that immature man was in the greatest danger. Sometimes when men say they are "listening to the Spirit" they are merely listening to their own emotions. We are not to add our feelings to Scripture. What does the Bible say? Every time it says the word "sinner" it is speaking your name. Every time it speaks of the blessings of those who believe then you should cry to God to give you the gift of faith. And do not stop praying until you know God has answered you. No additional words alleged to come from God bind our consciences so that we have to believe them. Our consciences are captive to the Word of God alone. It does not matter for our Christian lives if we never heard of one single "prophecy" or one "saying of Jesus" which was not found in the New Testament, or one so-called infallible utterance made by a pope, or if we never attended a revival where the greatest preacher in the world was preaching an inspiring sermon. It does not matter that we went through our entire lives and missed such words. We have "Moses and the prophets," and their words we must not miss out on. Every document placed alongside Scripture always fails to deemphasize the teachings of the Bible and to say things that are contrary to Scripture itself.

Thank God for the sufficiency of Scripture, and go out and live as if you truly believe in its sufficiency.

CHAPTER 6

The Inspiration, Infallibility, and Authority of Scripture

2 Peter 1:21

Gerald Bilkes

The subject before us is one that every man and woman needs to reckon with from the very outset of their lives; and if they never have, they need to now. It is one that makes a difference for time and eternity, for worship and work, for life and family, and for how we live every day.

It's a doctrine on which the church either stands or falls. If the Bible has the authority it says it has as the perfect word of God, the church is under its authority. If it does not, the church may be all sorts of things, but not a place where the Word of God is the ultimate authority.

The issue before us is one on which there are only two positions, though many imagine there are subtle refinements they can make. The issue is this: is the Bible our perfect authority, yes or no?

This is not a new issue, for it was the issue at the crossroads of Paradise, when the subtle serpent said to the woman, "Yea, hath God said, Ye shall not eat of every tree of the garden?" (Gen. 3:1).

Over the centuries, Satan's whisper has become a loud shout. J. I. Packer writes, "If I were the devil, one of my first aims would be to stop folk from digging into the Bible. I should do all I could to surround it with the spiritual equivalent of pits, thorns, hedges, and human traps to frighten people off."[1] Satan has not stopped and will not stop this attack on God. A. W. Pink wrote:

Every available weapon in the devil's arsenal has been employed in his determined and ceaseless efforts to destroy the temple of God's truth. In the first days of the Christian era

---

1. J. I. Packer, introduction to *Knowing Scripture*, by R.C. Sproul (Downers Grove: InterVarsity, 1979), 9.

the attack of the enemy was made openly—the bonfire being the chief instrument of destruction—but, in these "last days" the assault is made in a more subtle manner and comes from a more unexpected quarter. The divine origin of the Scriptures is now disputed in the name of "Scholarship" and "Science," and that, too, by those who profess to be friends and champions of the Bible. Much of the learning and theological activity of the hour, are concentrated in the attempt to discredit and destroy the authenticity and authority of God's Word, the result being that thousands of nominal Christians are plunged into a sea of doubt. Many of those who are paid to stand in our pulpits and defend the Truth of God are now the very ones who are engaged in sowing the seeds of unbelief and destroying the faith of those to whom they minister. But these modern methods will prove no more successful in their efforts to destroy the Bible than did those employed in the opening centuries of the Christian era. As well might the birds attempt to demolish the granite rock of Gibraltar by pecking at it with their beaks—"For ever, O Lord, thy Word is settled in heaven" (Ps. 119:89).[2]

Despite everything happening around us, we should remember that the faithful have always trusted the weight of their souls on Scripture. B. B. Warfield said it well:

Nor do we need to do more than remind ourselves that this attitude of entire trust in every word of the Scriptures has been characteristic of the people of God from the very foundation of the church. Christendom has always reposed upon the belief that the utterances of this book are properly oracles of God. The whole body of Christian literature bears witness to this fact. We may trace its stream to its source, and everywhere it is vocal with a living faith in the divine trustworthiness of the Scriptures of God in every one of their affirmations. This is the murmur of the little rills of Christian speech which find their tenuous way through the parched heathen land of the early second century. And this is the mighty voice of the great river

2. A. W. Pink, *The Divine Inspiration of the Bible* (Swengel, Pa.: Bible Truth Depot, 1917), 7.

of Christian thought which sweeps through the ages, freighted with blessings for men.[3]

How should we approach this topic of the authority of Scripture? Many people approach it in the wrong way. For example, some take up the question like this: "Can the Bible as it comes to us truly be an acceptable authority to us?" A variation of this approach is to ask: "What will happen to us if we bow to the authority of Scripture? What kinds of things will we be able to do and not do, think or not think?" And if we find that a stretch, we will reject the authority of Scripture or conceive of it in a way that will not infringe on our own sensibilities. A third way many investigate this question is to find out what people have done in the past, compare their views of authority to others' out there, and try to find a happy medium. A fourth way is to try to resolve all the problems that come at us if we were to posit the authority of Scripture, all the supposed contradictions, problems, and obstacles that would appear if we were to accept the complete authority of the Bible. J. Oswald Dykes said, "If men must have a reconciliation for all conflicting truths before they will believe any; if they must see how the promises of God are to be fulfilled before they will obey his commands; if duty is to hang upon the satisfying of the understanding, instead of the submission of the will,—then the greater number of us will find the road of faith and the road of duty blocked at the outset."[4]

What each of these vantage points has in common is that they begin with people. This way of trying to decide the issue will always fall short because then we are asked to judge God's authority, and being what we are by nature, fallen creatures, we will never climb up through our own reasoning to relinquish our own authority and bow under the authority of God.

So what must we do? The only proper approach to this topic is to take God at His Word. That means to hear what the Bible says about itself. That will put the issue to us, from the outset, not in a man-centered way, but in a God-centered way. In his excellent book, *Under God's Word*, J. I. Packer directs us to Psalm 119:34: "Give me

---

3. B. B. Warfield, Samuel G. Craig, and Cornelius Van Til, *The Inspiration and Authority of the Bible* (Philadelphia: Presbyterian and Reformed, 1948), 107.

4. J. Oswald Dykes, *Abraham, the Friend of God: a Study from Old Testament History* (London: James Nisbet, 1877), 257.

understanding, and I shall keep thy law; yea, I shall observe it with my whole heart."[5] Packer points out that this is the only place to start as we desire to understand the doctrine of Scripture. This prayer is an admission that of ourselves we lack the understanding we need to follow Scripture. We need an understanding greater than we ourselves can muster in order to embrace this Book and submit to its claims.

Essentially, the only other alternative to this prayer of the psalmist is to submit the Bible to our present, fallen understanding. And, as Packer points out,

> In that case Psalm 119 will stand as an everlasting rebuke to us: for instead of doubting and discounting some things in his Bible the Psalmist prayed for understanding so that he might live by God's law. This is the path of true reverence, true discipleship, and true enrichment. But once we entertain the needless and unproved, indeed unprovable, notion that Scripture cannot be fully trusted, that path is partly closed to us. Therefore, it is important to maintain inerrancy, and counter denials of it; for only so can we keep open the path of consistent submission to biblical authority, and consistently concentrate on the true problem, that of gaining understanding, without being entangled in the false question, how much of what Scripture asserts as true should we disbelieve?[6]

Or as Dr. Martyn Lloyd-Jones said, "Ultimately this question of the authority of the Scriptures is a matter of faith and not of argument."[7]

There are a number of biblical concepts that guard the authority of the Word of God. They are especially inspiration, infallibility or inerrancy, and authority. If the Bible is not inspired, contains mistakes, or isn't clear, it can't be authoritative. The questions then are exactly these: What does Scripture assert as true? What does Scripture say about itself? And flowing from that, what difference does that make in our lives?

The Inspiration of the Bible

It is of great significance that God speaks. Thus the first thing we need to settle is that God is a God who speaks. He spoke this world

---

5. J. I. Packer, *Under God's Word* (London: Lakeland, 1980), 19.
6. Packer, *Under God's Word*, 19.
7. D. Martyn Lloyd-Jones, "Authority of the Scriptures," *Decision* (June 1963).

into being. "Through faith we understand that the worlds were framed by the word of God, so that things which are seen were not made of things which do appear" (Heb. 11:3).

When He speaks He reveals Himself; that is why creation reveals God. As Psalm 19:1–2 says, "The heavens declare the glory of God, and the firmament sheweth his handywork. Day unto day uttereth speech, and night unto night sheweth knowledge." If we think about this first "book" of revelation which we call creation and providence, then the doctrine of inspiration is not so difficult to understand. If God can reveal Himself clearly in nature, how much more can He not reveal Himself in His own Word?

The doctrine of inspiration is most specifically taught in two great passages of Scripture: First, consider 2 Peter 1:21: "For the prophecy came not in old time by the will of man: but holy men of God spake as they were moved by the Holy Ghost." This passage emphasizes and explains the divine origin of prophecy, and, by extension, Scripture. Peter attributes the glory, uniqueness, and perfection of prophecy to the fact that God moves men to speak. Here is the biblical concept of inspiration: men were moved by God and spoke. They did not stop being men. They were men through and through; each human author is unique, with different capacities, capabilities, sensibilities, and so they spoke and wrote. They didn't draw or paint or sculpt or anything else. They spoke words, and they did so in a way that God was in control over them. He moved them. He overshadowed them. They opened their mouths because of Him. What they spoke was God's Word. They spoke what He wanted them to speak. They kept speaking as long as He wanted them to speak. They stopped when He directed them to stop. What they spoke was God's Word and the process made sure of that. Calvin added this: "He calls them the holy men of God, because they faithfully executed the office committed to them, having sustained the person of God in their ministrations. He says that they were [moved by the Holy Ghost]—not that they were bereaved of mind, (as the Gentiles imagined their prophets to have been,) but because they dared not to announce anything of their own, and obediently followed the Spirit as their guide, who ruled in their mouth as in his own sanctuary."[8]

---

8. John Calvin, *Commentaries on the Catholic Epistles*, trans. and ed. John Owen (Edinburgh: Calvin Translation Society, 1855), 391.

The second main proof for the doctrine of inspiration is 2 Timothy 3:16–17: "All scripture is given by inspiration of God, and is profitable for doctrine, for reproof, for correction, for instruction in righteousness: that the man of God may be perfect, throughly furnished unto all good works." Here we learn that Scripture was not dictated by God, but was inspired by God. He so moved upon the scriptural writers that what they wrote down conveyed His breath. The Word of God is the Word of the Spirit. That is why Scripture says, "as the Holy Ghost saith" (Heb. 3:7; cf. Rev. 2:29; 3:22).

Inspiration is not simply that these men through the help of God and His Spirit achieved something beyond the ordinary, as talented men, and that we now look at it and say that it's inspired, like we say of some piece of art or poetry that is sublime and extraordinary. Indeed, Scripture *is* extraordinary, but it is more. It is inspired by God.

Neither is this inspiration that God gave them merely thoughts, ideas, or concepts that they then spun according to their own abilities, like philosophers or poets with ideas impressed upon them who then take pen to paper and write something beautiful or influential. No, this is far too low a bar to use for comparison with the inspiration of Scripture.

Neither is inspiration those moments in which, while we read the Bible, the Lord gives us certain insights whereby we see that the things the Bible says are special. That is a different doctrine, the doctrine of illumination, which we also hold to and believe. It is an absolute requirement for anyone who will truly believe Scripture savingly that he or she must be illumined by the Spirit. However, *this* is not inspiration. The text says, "All Scripture is *given* by inspiration" (2 Tim. 3:16), not that all Scripture is *received* by inspiration.

Finally, inspiration doesn't mean that God dictated all the words to the authors of Scripture. There are times when the Lord did give exact messages, as you can find in the prophets, for example, when God tells Elijah to go to Ahab after he killed Naboth. It reads, "Arise, go down to meet Ahab king of Israel, which is in Samaria: behold, he is in the vineyard of Naboth, whither he is gone down to possess it. And thou shalt speak unto him, saying, Thus saith the LORD, Hast thou killed, and also taken possession? And thou shalt speak unto him, saying, Thus saith the LORD, In the place where dogs licked the blood of Naboth shall dogs lick thy blood, even thine" (1 Kings

21:18–19). So in certain cases, God dictated his Word to prophets. However, when Moses wrote the history of the world, the patriarchs, and Israel, God moved Him to write it. So too did He move Luke who wrote the history of Christ on earth; he researched it and God moved him to write it. Mechanical dictation could simply reach the outer ear of a prophet, but in the case of inspiration, God moved the whole prophet to speak and to write, all his personality, capacity, emotion, will, mind, and spirit.

Many have appropriately compared the human author to a musical instrument that someone plays. When someone extremely skilled takes hold of an organ, piano, or harp, he or she can produce very beautiful music, even if the instrument may be inferior. Of course, the comparison needs this caveat, that God—being almighty, all-wise, and in no way bound as we are—moved upon the human instruments in such a way that the words are flawless. I'll come back to that in a moment when we speak about infallibility, but allow me to elaborate on this by quoting the Princeton theologian B. B. Warfield:

> The Biblical books are called inspired as the Divinely determined products of inspired men; the Biblical writers are called inspired as breathed into by the Holy Spirit, so that the product of their activities transcends human powers and becomes Divinely authoritative. Inspiration is, therefore, usually defined as a supernatural influence exerted on the sacred writers by the Holy Spirit, by virtue of which their writings are given divine truthfulness, and constitute an infallible and sufficient rule of faith and practice.[9]

Elsewhere, Warfield wrote:

> What it says of Scripture is, not that it is "breathed into by God," or is the product of the Divine "inbreathing" into its human authors, but that it is breathed out by God, "God-breathed," the product of the creative breath of God. In a word, what is declared by this fundamental passage is simply that the Scriptures are a Divine product, without any indication of how God has operated in producing them. No term could have been chosen, however, which would have more emphatically asserted

---

9. B. B. Warfield, *The Inspiration and Authority of the Bible*, 131.

the Divine production of Scripture than that which is here employed."[10]

What a glorious thought. No wonder the doctrine of inspiration has been so celebrated in Protestant and Reformed churches. John Macleod, Principal of the Free College in Edinburgh, fittingly wrote in 1935:

> Now to those who hold with us this, the faith of the Reformed Churches, it sounds simply absurd to hear men describe the doctrine of inspiration as though it were an impossible thing for a transcendent sovereign God so to use a man in the full and free exercise of his faculties as an instrument of His own hand for making known His mind and will.... It is of the essence of stupidity not to see that God Almighty is not confined to a dead level of monotony when He is pleased to speak to His creatures in His written word. To say that inspiration of necessity suppresses the distinctive features of human expression when men are under its influence is to refuse to acknowledge that God is able to use men in the full and free exercise of their distinct individuality. It sets unwarrantable bounds to the power of Almighty God.[11]

The Infallibility of the Bible

Because it is God who inspires Scripture, it is an infallible or inerrant book. Both words mean essentially the same thing. Infallibility is a more classical term; inerrancy a more recent one. One of the reasons evangelicals started using the term "inerrancy" is because scholars tried to restrict the doctrine of the perfection of Scripture to issues of faith and life, not worldview or science, or they sought to limit it to what the authors *intended* to teach, and not what they supposedly didn't intend to teach, thereby narrowing the doctrine of the perfection of Scripture so that many things could be said to be mistakes. That is why in the last half century the term "inerrancy" has gained popularity, specifying that the Bible is accurate down to all its details. In other words, the Bible is absolutely without error.

---

10. B. B. Warfield, "Inspiration," in *The International Standard Bible Encyclopedia, Second Edition,* ed. Geoffrey W. Bromiley (Grand Rapids: Eerdmans, 1982), 2:840.

11. John Macleod, "The Inspiration of the Scriptures," *The Evangelical Quarterly* 7, no. 1 (Jan. 1935): 24–38.

The proof for this doctrine lies in Scripture itself. Scripture makes clear that it is infallible or inerrant with its very words. Consider the following texts:

- Numbers 23:19: "God is not a man, that he should lie; neither the son of man, that he should repent: hath he said, and shall he not do it? or hath he spoken, and shall he not make it good?"

- 2 Samuel 7:28: "And now, O LORD God, thou art that God, and thy words be true, and thou hast promised this goodness unto thy servant."

- Psalm 12:6: "The words of the LORD are pure words: as silver tried in a furnace of earth, purified seven times."

- Psalm 19:7a: "The law of the LORD is perfect, converting the soul."

- Proverbs 30:5: "Every word of God is pure: he is a shield unto them that put their trust in him" (see also, Ps. 119:140, 160).

Significantly, Christ Himself said to the religious leaders of His time, "Ye do err, not knowing the scriptures" (Matt. 22:29), which implies that Scripture is a standard that does not err. As additional proof, we find that Scripture everywhere treats the rest of the Scripture as inerrant. Christ famously said, "Till heaven and earth pass, one jot or one tittle shall in no wise pass from the law, till all be fulfilled" (Matt. 5:18). In other words, down to the very smallest details of the Word of God, nothing can be considered dispensable, inauthentic, or not worthy of our highest regard. Similarly, James says: "For whosoever shall keep the whole law, and yet offend in one point, he is guilty of all" (James 2:10). Finally, Revelation commands respect for the smallest details of the Word of God: "If any man shall add unto these things, God shall add unto him the plagues that are written in this book: And if any man shall take away from the words of the book of this prophecy, God shall take away his part out of the book of life, and out of the holy city, and from the things which are written in this book" (Rev. 22:18–19).

There is a text in the Bible that proves that its inspiration extends to the very words of the human authors, thus rendering Scripture inerrant down to its smallest detail. It is 1 Corinthians 2:12–13, where Paul writes, "Now we have received, not the spirit of the world, but the spirit which is of God; that we might know the things that are freely given to us of God. Which things also we speak, not in the words which man's wisdom teacheth, but which the Holy Ghost teacheth; comparing spiritual things with spiritual." From this text, we can see that it is the very words that we have on the pages of Scripture that are the words which the Spirit teaches. Every word of the Bible is God's word and is thus inerrant. Similarly, God says to Jeremiah, "I have put my words in thy mouth" (Jer. 1:9). And a few chapters later, He elaborates, "Behold, I will make my words in thy mouth fire, and this people wood, and it shall devour them" (Jer. 5:14).

The inerrancy of the Bible means that Scripture can be thoroughly trusted. It does not first need the approval of priests or popes, nor does it need the verification of science or archaeology to be trusted. No, it is thoroughly trustworthy from the outset, down to the details and right to the very end. How we need the blessed ministry of the Spirit, who illumines our darkened hearts and makes us receptive to the undiluted teaching of the Word of God regarding His inspiration and infallibility.

That doesn't mean that the Bible does not need to be interpreted. Christ commands us to "search the scriptures" (John 5:39). The Bible needs to be read, searched, and understood. Scripture must be compared with Scripture. There are figures of speech that the authors employ that need to be explained. Like ourselves, many times they use the language of observation. We need to interpret Scripture as it is designed to be interpreted, as the Spirit designed it to be read, uncovering the meaning, the proper and singular meaning of it at every point. There are many things that need to be harmonized, some with difficulty from our perspective, but none of them detract from the scriptural doctrine of inspiration and infallibility.

In this connection, Warfield helpfully observed:

> Even a detailed attempt to explain away the texts which teach the doctrine of the plenary inspiration and unvarying truth of Scripture, involves the admission that in their obvious meaning such texts teach the doctrine which it is sought to explain away.... It is doubtless the profound and ineradicable conviction, so expressed, of the need of an infallible Bible, if men are to seek and find salvation in God's announced purpose of grace, and peace and comfort in his past dealings with his people,

that has operated to keep the formulas of the churches and the hearts of the people of God, through so many ages, true to the Bible doctrine of plenary inspiration. In that doctrine men have found what their hearts have told them was the indispensable safeguard of a sure word of God to them,—a word of God to which they could resort with confidence in every time of need, to which they could appeal for guidance in every difficulty, for comfort in every sorrow, for instruction in every perplexity; on whose "Thus saith the Lord" they could safely rest all their aspirations and all their hopes. Such a Word of God, each one of us knows he needs—not a Word of God that speaks to us only through the medium of our fellow-men, men of like passions and weaknesses with ourselves, so that we have to feel our way back to God's Word through the church, through tradition, or through apostles, standing between us and God; but a Word of God in which God speaks directly to each of our souls. Such a Word of God, Christ and his apostles offer us, when they give us the Scriptures, not as man's report to us of what God says, but as the very Word of God itself, spoken by God himself through human lips and pens. Of such a precious possession, given to her by such hands, the church will not lightly permit herself to be deprived.[12]

Therefore, there may be no whittling away at this doctrine of the inspiration and infallibility of Scripture, but we must bow under it and submit to the authority of the God who speaks in His Word in every word.

The Authority of the Bible

The inspiration and infallibility of Scripture mean it is authoritative. We need to believe it, practice it, and spread it as the ultimate authority for everyone and on everything. No human government has authority to go against the Word of God, for it has infinitely greater authority than the highest earthly authority imaginable. We ought to treat it as the angels do every word that comes from their Sovereign, and even note the regard that the devil and demons have for the powerful Word of God. Let's unpack our duty vis-à-vis the Word of God in five applicatory thoughts.

---

12. B. B. Warfield, "The Inspiration of the Bible," *Bibliotheca Sacra* 51 (1894): 628–35.

It has authority to demolish the wisdom of the world.

Because of that, we need to cast aside as folly any and all of the wisdom of the world that militates against the Word of God. As Paul writes in 1 Corinthians: "But we speak the wisdom of God in a mystery, even the hidden wisdom, which God ordained before the world unto our glory: which none of the princes of this world knew: for had they known it, they would not have crucified the Lord of glory. But as it is written, Eye hath not seen, nor ear heard, neither have entered into the heart of man, the things which God hath prepared for them that love him. But God hath revealed them unto us by his Spirit: for the Spirit searcheth all things, yea, the deep things of God. For what man knoweth the things of a man, save the spirit of man which is in him? even so the things of God knoweth no man, but the Spirit of God" (1 Cor. 2:7–11).

It has authority to bring life from the dead.

The apostle writes, "The word of God is quick [living], and powerful, and sharper than any twoedged sword, piercing even to the dividing asunder of soul and spirit, and of the joints and marrow, and is a discerner of the thoughts and intents of the heart" (Heb. 4:12). We cannot hide from God's Word.

God's Word separates. It separates that which is from us and that which is from God. It takes away everything that needs to go and replaces it with godliness. It is as if we are lying on an operating table and we have become exposed, as the Word of God has cut us open to see how we function and operate. But then God heals us again; He heals the wounds after taking the problems out and fixing our bodies from the inside out. For God's Word breaks, but heals again. "See now that I, even I, am he, and there is no god with me: I kill, and I make alive; I wound, and I heal: neither is there any that can deliver out of my hand" (Deut. 32:39).

When you cast aside all else and come under Scripture, you will find, as Spurgeon said, "The Word of God is so sharp a thing, so full of cutting power, that you may be bleeding under its wounds before you have seriously suspected the possibility of such a thing."[13] Or as he said elsewhere, "Take up any other book except the Bible and

---

13. C. H. Spurgeon, "The Word a Sword," *Metropolitan Tabernacle Pulpit* (Edinburgh: Banner of Trust, 1970), 34:115–16.

there may be a measure of power in it, but there is not that inde-
scribable vitality in it which breathes and speaks—and pleads and
conquers in the case of this sacred volume."[14]

The Bible is a book that is applicable for all times, every age,
every person, and has forever worked with its changing power. It is
living and powerful. Even if you feel dead when you start reading it,
it will revive your soul. Spurgeon wrote, "You need not bring life to
the Scripture. You shall draw life from the Scripture."[15]

It has authority to transform our lives.
God's Word can change the hardest of people. Paul writes, "For our
gospel came not unto you in word only, but also in power, and in
the Holy Ghost, and in much assurance" (1 Thess. 1:5a). Psalm 107:20
says: "He sent his word, and healed them, and delivered them from
their destructions." We can depend on the power of the Word for
transformation. "For as the rain cometh down, and the snow from
heaven, and returneth not thither, but watereth the earth, and
maketh it bring forth and bud, that it may give seed to the sower,
and bread to the eater: so shall my word be that goeth forth out of
my mouth: it shall not return unto me void, but it shall accomplish
that which I please, and it shall prosper in the thing whereto I sent
it" (Isa. 55:10–11). As Martin Luther said, "Christ is involved in the
Scriptures as a body in its clothes."[16] He does this powerful work
by regenerating the soul, not of perishable seed but of imperishable,
through the Word of God that abides forever (1 Peter 1:23). It unbinds
the fettered sinner and he is freed by the truth, for the truth sets him
free, if he continues in the Word (John 8:31–36). We must continue to
come under the Word. It will sanctify us as Christ prays, "Sanctify
them through thy truth; thy word is truth" (John 17:17).

It has the authority to resist Satan.
"For we wrestle not against flesh and blood, but against principalities, against powers, against the rulers of the darkness of this world,
against spiritual wickedness in high places. Wherefore take unto you

---

14. Spurgeon, "The Word a Sword," *Metropolitan Tabernacle Pulpit,* 34:112.
15. Spurgeon, "The Word a Sword," *Metropolitan Tabernacle Pulpit,* 34:113.
16. Erwin W. Lutzer, *Seven Reasons Why You Can Trust the Bible* (Chicago: Moody, 2008), 43.

the whole armour of God…and take the helmet of salvation, and the sword of the Spirit, which is the word of God" (Eph. 6:12–13a, 17). So Christ resisted Satan with the words, "Man shall not live by bread alone, but by every word that proceedeth out of the mouth of God" (Matt. 4:4). "Then the devil leaveth him" (Matt. 4:11).

It has authority to deal with suffering and death.
Christ Himself quoted Scripture, bringing it to mind on the cross, confiding in Scripture, pleading it. Paul asked for the parchments (2 Tim. 4:13), likely copies of portions of Scripture.

When Sir Walter Scott, himself a famed author, lay dying, he called his secretary and asked him for "The Book." And when his secretary brought to mind the thousands of books in Scott's library, he asked which book. "The Book," replied Scott. "The Bible—the only book for a dying man."[17]

Conclusion

I ask you, in closing, do you hold by gracious faith unwaveringly to what Scripture says about itself? It is the word of God, inspired, infallible, inerrant, down to its very words, and authoritative. When you hold to this by saving faith, you can rest in an unshakeable certainty in life and in death.

---

17. John MacArthur, *How to Study the Bible* (Chicago: Moody, 2009), 8.

THE BEAUTIFUL LIFE OF FEEDING ON GOD'S WORD

CHAPTER 7

Holding Fast to the Word of Life

Philippians 2:14–16

Ronald Kalifungwa

About four or five years after his last visit to Philippi, while a prisoner at Rome, Paul received a delegation from the Philippian church. The Philippians had generously supported Paul in the past. Now hearing of Paul's imprisonment they sent another contribution to him and, along with it, Epaphroditus, to minister to Paul's needs. Unfortunately, Epaphroditus suffered a near-fatal illness either while en route to Rome or after he arrived. Accordingly, Paul decided to send Epaphroditus back to Philippi and wrote a letter to the Philippians to send back with him.

Paul had several purposes to serve in composing this letter. To start, he wanted to express in writing his thanks for the Philippians' gift. He also wanted the Philippians to know why he decided to return Epaphroditus to them so they would not think his service to Paul had been unsatisfactory. In addition, he wanted to inform them about his circumstances in Rome, to exhort them, and to warn them against false teachers.

Among the exhortations Paul laid before the Philippians was the call to hold fast to the word of life in the midst of a crooked and perverse nation (Phil. 2:15–16), which highlights the following three points.

The Context in Which They Were to Shine as Lights, Holding Fast to the Word of Life

In Philippians 2, Paul describes the context in terms of a generation or nation characterized by crookedness and perversity. "Crooked" means "warped" or "winding;" "perversion" means "distortion" (v. 15). The two words together describe a nation that is not morally straight but is, rather, given to moral corruption. In the book of Philippians, Paul mentions three immoral habits that concretized this crookedness and perversity.

Murmuring and Disputing (Phil. 2:14)

To murmur is to complain. Murmuring implies an open, audible grumbling which may include an impatient criticism. Disputing (*dialogismos* in Greek) referred to haggling, confrontation, and even litigation in court. Paul's use of the word probably relates to an attitude of the heart that was confrontational. He is saying this generation loved to grumble and argue. They murmured about everything: against God and Christ, against ministers of the gospel, and against one another. Paul seems to have considered this inappropriate and possibly an intellectual rebellion against God. No wonder he urges the Philippians to do everything without murmuring and disputing.

Enmity to the Cross (Phil. 3:18)

The Jewish false teachers were among the bitterest foes of the gospel. Paul refers to them as "the enemies of the cross of Christ." They were open and implacable enemies of the crucified Christ. They esteemed not Jesus and anathematized Him and His followers. To them the preaching of Christ crucified was an offence and a stumbling block (1 Cor. 1:23). They therefore shunned it, preferring rather to preach circumcision and righteousness through works of the law as necessary to salvation. In this way they emptied the cross of its power and rendered it ineffectual to the souls of men. They also tried actively to prevent the spread of the gospel. Paul was in prison as he wrote this letter because they would not allow him to preach the cross.

Contrariness to the Demands of the Gospel (Phil. 3:19)

This contrariness to the demands of the gospel is identified in three ways.

First, they served their own bellies. That is to say, they placed confidence in the observance of laws regarding meats and drinks and not in the law of the gospel which consists of "righteousness, and peace, and joy in the Holy Ghost" (Rom. 14:17).

Second, they gloried in their shame. This means that they were proud about the evil practices which they committed in secret, their crafty walking and deceitful handling of the Word of God (2 Cor. 4:2), and their idolatry.

Third, they minded earthly things. They were concerned with worldly things such as pleasure, popularity, and riches; they sought their own things rather than the things of Christ.

Simply put, this context was comprised of a generation in darkness. This is suggested in Philippians 2:15 in which that generation or nation is contrasted with the Philippians who were to shine as lights in the world. A generation in darkness is intellectually ignorant. It is particularly blinded to the gospel and to the ways of God (2 Cor. 4:4). And where there is intellectual darkness, there will be the works of that darkness such as debauchery, immorality, shamelessness, strife, and envy. So on the one hand you have the intellectual side of darkness, the lack of knowing God or His truth, and on the other, the results of that noetic darkness, namely the deeds of that darkness, moral evil.

The nation in which the Philippians existed is very similar to ours, isn't it? Our generation is increasingly rejecting of the light, preferring to love darkness instead. The consequence of this self-imposed ignorance is that millions of people today live in the darkness of witchcraft, drugs, alcohol, violence, gambling, lying, and stealing. Many feel that there is nothing wrong with fornication, adultery, homosexuality, abortion (murder), hatred, prejudice, planting bombs, shooting people, or failing to serve the living God. Right has become wrong and wrong has become right. The woe expressed in Isaiah 5:20 would be a fitting expression of our generation: "Woe unto them that call evil good, and good evil; that put darkness for light, and light for darkness; that put bitter for sweet, and sweet for bitter!" Such was the context in which the Philippians were to shine as lights, holding fast to the word of life.

The Shining They Were to Display in Such a Crooked and Perverse Generation

"To shine" means "to be bright or resplendent." The Philippians were shining and were to continue to shine as lights in a darkened generation. Notice that they were not to accommodate the darkness or to become like the darkness; they were to shine as lights in the darkness. There are two questions I would like us to answer regarding their shining as lights.

Why They Shined as Lights
First, light is undefiled even when it comes into contact with the foulest pollution and enters into the innermost recesses of darkness and rottenness. It retains the same amount of light, taking on no darkness, contracting no stain, remaining bright and unmarred. In a sense therefore true light is incapable of being defiled. That is why Paul proposes that they shine as lights. He wanted them to remain untainted by the corrupt generation that surrounded them.

Second, light overcomes darkness when it comes into contact with it. This is well illustrated in Genesis 1:3 (see also 2 Cor. 4:6) in which, at God's command, darkness was displaced by shining light. Paul opines that they were displacing the darkness by shining, and also implies that they should continue to overcome the darkness of their generation by their shining as lights.

How They Shined as Lights
First, they would do so by revealing or exposing the darkness by denouncing it. Here they did the work of a lighthouse keeper, who is there on a dangerous coast to warn vessels of their peril and to save them from shipwreck. Even so the light of Christians is intended to be a beacon that guides and gives hope to others.

Second, they would shine by their good deeds (Matt. 5:14). Paul particularly refers to the need for them to reveal their blamelessness (irreproachableness) and harmlessness (innocence) in Phil. 2:15. This is another way of speaking about being holy or pure, as light is, so they might be examples of how life should be lived and also move their generation to glorify God our Father in heaven.

The Holding Forth of the Word of Life and Its Relationship to the Act of Shining as Lights in the World

The connection between the phrases "ye shine as lights in the world" in verse 15 and "holding forth the word of life" in verse 16 is that Christians shine as lights (that is, like stars in the night sky) in a crooked and perverse generation by holding forth the word of life. This raises the question, what does it mean to "hold forth the word of life"? We will begin by looking at the meaning of the statement "the word of life." This reference to the gospel, or to the Word of God, is associated with life because life and all that it implies—power, health, and fruitfulness—are mediated from God to man through his Word. When we stay away from the Word our souls languish. Life is like the wick of a lamp. If you starve the wick of your lamp by not soaking it in fuel, the light will grow dim and eventually die. On the other hand, if you do soak it in fuel, it burns and shines ever so brightly, giving light to the room. In the same way, the Word of God is the fuel of our lives. If you keep your life (wick) in the Word (fuel), holding it fast, your life will flourish because the Word is the health of your life.

Second, let's examine the phrase "holding fast." These words are translated from a Greek word that means "to retain one's position," "to detain one's gaze," or "to keep one's gaze in official custody." In Acts 19:22 it's translated, "he [Paul] himself *stayed* [held his place] in Asia for a season." In 1 Timothy 4:16, the same root word which is translated as holding fast in Philippians 2:16 is translated as "take heed unto thyself, and unto the doctrine."

The point of Philippians 2:15–16 therefore is that they must hold their gaze on, must hold their position with, and must not leave the word of life. They must stay with the word of life, fixing their minds on it. Staying with the word of life is what will keep their spiritual lives shining—that is to say, healthy and strong—and will keep their witness to a dark and dying generation effective.

The truth of Romans 3:10–18 is becoming ever so stark: "There is none righteous, no, not one: there is none that understandeth, there is none that seeketh after God. They are all gone out of the way, they are together become unprofitable; there is none that doeth good, no, not one. Their throat is an open sepulchre; with their tongues they have used deceit; the poison of asps is under their lips: whose mouth is full of cursing and bitterness: their feet are swift to shed blood: destruction and misery are in their ways: and the way of peace have they not known: there is no fear of God before their eyes." During this time when our generation is fast moving from one degree of darkness to the next, we too need to stay with the word of life. That is what will keep our spiritual lives shining.

Motivations for Holding Fast to the Word of Life

There is a sevenfold motivation to hold fast to the word of life.

First of all, hold fast to the word of life because it generates faith. Romans 10:17 says, "Faith cometh by hearing, and hearing by the word of God." The Bible furthermore reminds us that without faith no one can please God (Heb. 11:6). If you believe in God and wish to please Him your whole life, hold fast to the word of life!

Second, hold fast to the word of life because it is the medium of the Holy Spirit's work. Paul asks the Galatians, "He therefore that ministereth to you the Spirit, and worketh miracles among you, doeth he it by the works of the law, or by the hearing of faith?" (Gal. 3:5). The answer Paul expects is that it was by the hearing of faith. If you would receive the Holy Spirit for the sanctification of your soul, hold fast to the word of life!

Third, hold fast to the word of life because it communicates life. The Lord says in Matthew 4:4, "Man shall not live by bread alone, but by every word that proceedeth out of the mouth of God." If you would live—really live—hold fast to the word of life!

Fourth, hold fast to the word of life because it brings freedom. Our Lord said in John 8:31–32, "If ye continue in my word…ye shall know the truth, and the truth shall make you free." If you would be free from your burden of ignorance, hold fast to the word of life!

Fifth, hold fast to the word of life because it leads to holiness. Jesus prays in John 17:17, "Sanctify them through thy truth: thy word is truth." If you would be empowered to say no to worldly passions and yes to godliness, self-control, and Christlikeness, hold fast to the word of life!

Sixth, hold fast to the word of life because it is the means to obtaining joy. Psalm 19:8 reminds us that the law of the Lord is able to make our hearts rejoice. If you would have joy—real and wonderful joy—hold fast to the word of life!

And last, hold fast to the word of life because it is the way to true fruitfulness. In Psalm 1:2–3, this is the promise to anyone whose delight is in the law of the Lord and on whose law one meditates day and night: "He shall be like a tree planted by the rivers of water, that bringeth forth his fruit in his season; his leaf also shall not wither; and whatsoever he doeth shall prosper." If therefore you would be strong, stable, and fruitful, hold fast to the word of life!

Conclusion

In light of all this, three exhortations are fitting in regard to the place of the word of life in our lives:

First, we must not be swept away by the waves of higher criticism, cultural relativism, and pragmatism, whose mission it is to remove the clarity, authority, and sufficiency of Scripture. Rather let us hold fast to the word of life as to a surfing board among tumultuous waves. It will save our lives.

Second, we must not be drowned in the seas of latitudinarianism and libertarianism, whose mission it is to undermine God's right to impose His will upon His creatures and upon His church. Let us strive to remain afloat by holding fast to the word of life, which is essentially our life belt.

Third, we must know what it is that Paul, through his words to the Philippians, calls us to hold fast to: the word of life. To know it, we must read it, listen to it, understand it, memorize it, and meditate on it. The results can only be beneficial. Our text suggests that we will profit from the Word by way of enjoying a vital relationship with God and building a character that is Christlike and which alone can enable us to shine as lights among this crooked and perverse generation.

CHAPTER 8

The Word of God and the Making of the Man of God

2 Timothy 3:15–17

Ronald Kalifungwa

If you have read through Paul's second epistle to Timothy, you will no doubt know that he wrote it while he was alone in prison. Prior to his incarceration, he seems to have been on a short visit to Troas where he was suddenly arrested and taken to Rome and imprisoned there. It was while waiting in this Roman dungeon, in chains and with no hope of deliverance, abandoned by virtually all those close to him for fear of persecution and imminent execution, that he wrote this letter to Timothy.

Why did Paul write to this young minister of the gospel? Well, Paul seems to have had reason to fear that Timothy was in danger of weakening spiritually. This would have been a grave concern for him since Timothy was earmarked to carry on Paul's work. He therefore writes to exhort him to "stir up" his gift, to replace fear with power, love, and a sound mind, to not be ashamed of Paul and the Lord, to willingly suffer for the gospel, to hold on to the truth, and to preach the word. To put it in a nutshell, the apostle encouraged him on many topics of perennial significance. It is not my intention now to discuss all of these topics. Rather, what I want to do is to outline for us the role of the Word in making Timothy a man of God.

Paul, in this second letter to Timothy, describes some false men of God with whom Timothy had to contend. He describes them as men who resist the truth: "men of corrupt minds, reprobate concerning the faith" (2 Tim. 3:8). He also describes them as men "who concerning the truth have erred" and men "who overthrow the faith of some" (2 Tim. 2:18).

In contrast to this, Timothy, a reserved and timid young man no older than his late teens to early twenties, is held up as a faithful man. Paul on more than one occasion in his two epistles to Timothy refers to him as a man of God.

Shaping Influences on Timothy

But how did Timothy become a man of God? A study of the two letters addressed to him suggests that there were several shaping influences that made him into the man of God he became. There was first the influence of his mother, Eunice, and possibly his grandmother, Lois. They both had a lively faith in the Lord and were known for their piety. Paul suggests that they had a spiritual influence on Timothy (2 Tim. 1:5). Then there was the influence of Paul himself. It appears that Timothy came to the knowledge of the Lord through Paul's ministry. Paul consequently referred to him as "my own son in the faith" (1 Tim. 1:2). So close was Paul's relationship to Timothy that he entrusted him with missions of great importance and also coauthored some letters with him. It is no wonder that Paul writes of Timothy, "I have no man likeminded" (Phil. 2:20). It is therefore not surprising that when Paul was in prison and awaiting martyrdom, he summoned his faithful friend, Timothy, for a last farewell. Paul's influence is unmistakable.

There was, finally, the influence of the Word of God (Scripture) on Timothy, and this of course is what I want us to consider. It seems that Paul, in identifying Timothy as a man of God and in counseling him to be a man of God, places a high premium on the role Scripture plays in realizing and maintaining this ideal. Paul therefore outlines a four-point process that culminated into making Timothy the man of God he became.

Timothy Was Acquainted with Scripture from Childhood

This is no doubt what laid the foundation for Timothy to become a man of God. Paul does not make certain at precisely what age Timothy was first instructed in Scripture. What he does make clear is that Timothy was a child, for the Greek word translated "child" means "a babe" or "an infant" (v. 15). It would appear therefore that he was taught Scripture as soon as he was capable of learning anything.

I imagine that his mother and possibly his grandmother taught him the Word diligently. They talked of it in their house, when they walked by the way, when they lay down, and when they rose. They would have bound the Word on their hands, and would also have seen to it that it was as frontlets between his eyes. As good guardians, they would have written the words on the door posts of their house and on their gate (Deut. 6:4–9). The intention of course was to acquaint him with Scripture. They wanted him to see, to pay attention to, and to be influenced by Scripture, and peradventure to be made wise unto salvation. This acquaintance with Scripture no doubt sowed the seeds that gave birth to the man of God, Timothy.

Timothy Was Made Wise unto Salvation by Scripture
Timothy did not become wise unto salvation of himself. He could not. None of us can. Left to himself he might have pursued the way of the Gentiles which would have led him into idolatry and an empty way of living. Or he might have pursued the way of most Jews which had a form of godliness but lacked the power thereof. Rather, Scripture made him wise unto salvation (2 Tim. 3:15).

In Psalm 19:7–8, David speaks of Scripture as possessing the ability to make wise the simple and to enlighten the eyes. The simple are those who are children in mind, silly or foolish. But Scripture is able to make them wise and noble.

Scripture makes the simple wise by giving them understanding, knowledge, and light. Timothy was made wise unto salvation when he heard Paul preach the gospel. That is to say, the Holy Spirit removed the veil (the foolishness that would have previously hidden Christ from Timothy's eyes), and given him understanding, knowledge, and light about Christ. Consequently, he looked to Christ's righteousness for justification, to His blood for peace, pardon, and cleansing, to His sacrifice for atonement, and to His fullness of grace for continual supply, eternal life, and glory. This knowledge opened the way for him to know God, to come to God, to walk with God, and to become a man of God. In other words, to have the life of a man of God, Timothy began with faith which comes by hearing of Christ in Scripture (Rom. 10:17).

Timothy Was Charged to Equip Himself for Every Good Work
by Availing Himself of Scripture
Second Timothy 3:17 suggests that the man of God has a good work to do. It is a work because it involves laboring in every part and

branch of the ministry. It is good because it is intrinsically right and virtuous, and because it benefits those for whom it is done. A major part of that good work consists in teaching, reproving, correcting, and training others in righteousness (2 Tim. 3:16).

To do this work the man of God must be "perfect" (complete) and "throughly furnished" (fully equipped). The words "perfect" and "furnished" refer to something to which nothing needs to be added in order to make it complete. The question is how such perfecting and equipping of the man of God might be attained.

Paul teaches that it is by the God-breathed Word, or Scripture. Paul writes concerning Scripture that it is profitable (v. 16). In other words, it is helpful or serviceable in positioning Timothy to do the good work. And the reason Paul assigns for Scripture's ability to do this is that it is God-breathed (v. 16a), a fact that identifies Scripture to be the very Word of God. Paul's point in 2 Timothy 3:16–17 therefore seems to be that because Scripture is the Word of God, it has the ingredients, namely, authority and sufficiency, to equip the man of God for the good work God has called him to do: to teach, rebuke, correct, and train men in righteousness. The use of the Word under the Spirit's power is how the man of God perfects and equips himself to effectively serve God.

Timothy Was Charged to Fulfill His Ministry through the
Exposition and Application of Scripture
This is essentially what constituted Timothy's primary work as a man of God. This work is summarized in the word "preach." Timothy was to preach the word (2 Tim. 4:2). Preaching presupposes three things.

First, the preacher or the man of God should have a passion for acquiring the mind of God. The implication of the foregoing is that before he presents the Word to the people of God, he must first himself receive it from God in a manner similar to the way the prophets of the Old Testament did. God sovereignly raised up these prophets to act as his mouthpiece. They were, metaphorically speaking, "the mouth of the LORD" (cf. Ex. 4:11–16). The prophet did not communicate the word of God before he received it.

Similarly, the man of God today must first hear from God. He does not do this through receiving inspiration via witchcraft-type divination, nor through the so-called revelation knowledge (Gnosticism) characteristic of the present-day faith charismatic movement. Rather, he does so through searching and assimilating Scripture, which is God's Word, and through submitting to the illuminating power of the Holy Spirit. This search and assimilation of God's Word ought to have two essential elements to it if it would assist the man of God to effectively acquire the mind of God.

1) It ought to be done prayerfully and meditatively. The man of God must pray for light and illumination. He must pray sincerely and sensibly with energy, warmth, and spirituality. He must also meditate upon the Word of God. Psalm 1:2–3 speaks of the blessedness of the man who meditates upon the Word day and night. Thomas Watson noted that "reading without meditation is barren, and meditation without reading is erroneous."[1] The man of God must therefore let his thoughts dwell upon the most material passages of Scripture. Again, Watson puts it well: "Meditation is the concoction of Scripture; reading brings a truth into our head, meditation brings it into our hearts.... Meditation without reading is erroneous; reading without meditation is barren. The bee sucks the flower, and then works it into the hive, and so turns it into honey; by reading we suck the flower of the word, by meditation we work it into the hive of our mind, and so it turns to profit. Meditation is the bellows of the affection. Psalm 119:8: 'While I was musing the fire burned.' The reason we come away so cold from reading the word, is because we do not warm ourselves at the fire of meditation."[2]

2) It ought to involve an exegetical study of the Word of God. The man of God must carefully investigate the original meaning of texts in their historical and literary contexts and he must draw from the texts their God-given meaning. To read his own opinions into the text is not an honorable thing for a man of God to do. He is a man of God; he must acquire the mind of God from His own Word. Paul speaks to this issue when he urges Timothy, "study [be diligent] to shew thyself approved unto God, a workman that needeth not to be ashamed, rightly dividing the word of truth" (2 Tim 2:15). According to this verse, a man of God must handle the Word of God properly through

---

1. Thomas Watson, *The Bible and the Closet* (Harrisonburg, Virginia: Sprinkle Publications, 1992), 24.
2. Watson, *The Bible and the Closet*, 24–25.

diligent study. If he doesn't, he has reason to be ashamed and he is not a true man of God.

Second, the preacher or man of God should display the character of God. In other words, he must display a high level of the virtues of godliness, righteousness, and holiness among others. The man of God represents God; he must reflect not only His mind but His character too. The Bible sets forth a cause-and-effect relationship between what a man of God is as a man and what he accomplishes as a minister of the Word. Paul speaks to this issue in 1 Thessalonians 1:4–5. Generally speaking, sustained effectiveness in pastoral ministry will be realized in direct proportion to the health and vigor of the whole redeemed humanity of the man of God.[3]

It is, I believe, for this reason that Paul urges Timothy to be an example to the believers "in word, in conversation, in charity [love], in spirit, in faith, in purity" (1 Tim. 4:12). Furthermore, in 1 Timothy 6:3, 11, and 14, Paul calls Timothy to flee from a life that does not accord with the words of our Lord Jesus Christ and to adorn the gospel with a life of obedience to the Lord's Word—a life which manifests in righteousness, godliness, faith, love, patience, and meekness.

Third, the preacher or man of God should display the mind of God. The word translated "preach" (*kērussō*) in 2 Timothy 4:2 means "to herald" or "to proclaim after the manner of a herald." The word "preach" always carries the suggestion of formality, gravity, and an authority which must be listened to and obeyed. In this manner, John the Baptist, Jesus our Lord, the apostles, and other Christian leaders preached. Paul charges Timothy to do the same.

Steven J. Lawson, in his book entitled *Famine in the Land*, defines preaching as "the man of God opening the word and expounding its truths so that the voice of God may be heard, the glory of God seen, and the will of God obeyed."[4]

In terms of Lawson's definition, the man of God must do what Ezra and the scribes did in Nehemiah 8:8. They read from the Law of God, sharing its meaning so that the people could hear and understand the voice of God. The man of God must preach in such a way that the glory of God is seen. In John the Baptist's style, the man of

---

3. Al Martin, "Pastoral Theology" lectures.
4. Steven J. Lawson, *Famine in the Land: A Passionate Call for Expository Preaching* (Chicago: Moody, 2003), 18.

God must decrease and Jesus, who is the exact representation of the image and glory of God, must increase (John 3:30). The task of the man of God is to be the bridegroom's friend: to prepare the way for Him, to make His voice louder, and to make Him increase in the eyes of the world. Ministers of the Word are only morning stars; Christ is the sun. As the stars gradually fade away to give way to the sun after the break of day, those of us who are preachers must pale away and become invisible before the superior brightness of Christ. When the man of God has preached to the people, there must be a sense and an urge in them to want to say, "The LORD, he is the God; the LORD, he is the God" (1 Kings 18:39

Last, in term of Lawson's definition, the man of God must preach in such a way that the will of God is obeyed. There is a cause-and-effect relationship between seeing God in His glory and seeing His Word as authoritative (2 Tim. 3:16a) and wanting to obey it. If people who listen to preachers don't see God as supreme and as One who is free to impose His will upon them, they will not have any sense of obligation to obey His will. Biblical preaching must therefore authoritatively declare the will of God, as reflected in the preacher's text, as well as authoritatively (and possibly gently and persuasively) call for belief, submission, and obedience to that will. Ultimately, this is what preaching is about—preachers becoming the mouthpiece of God so people, whatever condition they may be in, may respond to it in a way that honors Christ.

To secure submission and obedience, the man of God must preach in an applicatory way. In his book *Preaching Pure and Simple*, Stuart Olyott writes in regard to this, "Where there is no application, preaching has no soul, no life and no interest. It carries no striking convictions to the conscience and no healing comfort to the heart. It leaves each hearer feeling like a child who has never been hugged and who has never been [spanked]. Poor child! Whatever will become of him? He will go through life bewildered and disturbed, without moorings and without values."[5]

I believe that this is what Paul was expecting Timothy to do when he charged him to "preach the word" (the mind of God) to the people and to correctly divide it (2 Tim. 4:2; 2:15). He was to preach the

---

5. Stuart Olyott, *Preaching Pure and Simple* (Bridgend, Wales: Bryntirion Press, 2005), 114.

word with a view to instructing the people in the things of God, correcting them where they might have erred, reproving them where they might have strayed from the things of God, and training them in righteousness and Christlikeness (2 Tim. 3:16) where they might have needed to form habits of godly and Christlike men. For Timothy to preach this way would be for him to be an accomplished man of God.

Conclusion

The point of this message is that the Word of God under the power of the Spirit makes men who have the gifting and are called of God to become true men of God. This being the case, if those of us who call ourselves preachers would be men of God like Timothy, we must have a fourfold attitude toward the Word of God.

First, we must expose ourselves to the Word of God. We must read it, study it, meditate on it, and memorize it. It will make us wise, enlighten our eyes, rejoice our hearts, and equip us to be a blessing to people. The psalmist says in regard to the laws of God, "in keeping of them there is great reward" (Ps. 19:11).

Second, we must expose people to the Word of God if we would make people of God out of them. We must expose children to the Word of God, in a manner similar to the way Eunice and Lois prepared Timothy "from a child" to recognize the Messiah when He appeared (2 Tim. 3:15) by teaching him the Old Testament, such that when Paul came preaching Christ he, by the Spirit's grace, readily believed in the Savior. Even so we must teach Scripture to our children. Only Scripture under God can make them wise unto salvation.

We must expose young people to the Word of God. A young man can cleanse his way by heeding the Word of God (Psalm 119:9). We must expose all people to the Word of God, whoever they are, whatever condition they mind find themselves in. This is what will change, sanctify, and revive them.

Third, we must protect people against Word-sapping innovations such as entertainment in the context of worship. The music, the skits, the multimedia—these have become the means of taking the church back to the Dark Ages. As men of God, we must inoculate our flocks against things which leave our people with less of an appetite for the Word of God.

Last, we must adorn the Word we preach with a Word-inspired, godly life. We must live our lives in such a Christlike way that people will have no doubt that, via the Word and Spirit, a man of God has been made among them.

The flock of God also has a responsibility to pray and seek men who have under God been made men of God through the Word. Only such men can help to fulfill the end for which God has saved them, namely, conformity to Christ and the promotion of His glory.

CHAPTER 9

Finding Joy in God's Word

Psalm 119

David Murray

Psalm 119 is one long and exuberant song of delight in God's Word. Multiple descriptions of God's Word are punctuated with repeated exultations of joy in God's Word (Ps. 119:14, 16, 24, 35, 47, 70, 77, 92, 111, 143, 162, 174).

My favorite line is, "I rejoice at thy word, as one that findeth great spoil" (v. 162). I love the imagery of someone who turns a corner one day only to find a huge pile of treasure left behind by a marauding army, and it's all his. Can you imagine what that would feel like? That's how we should feel when we open the Bible. Charles Bridges wrote, "Often had David found great spoil in his many wars, but never had his greatest victories brought him such rich spoil as he had now discovered in the Word of God."[1]

To help you find joy in God's Word, I want to give you twenty-five exhortations to rejoice in God's Word, twenty-five ways that you should seek to find joy in it. Then I will give an example of how God's Word can bring joy to you even when you are sad and depressed.

An Exhortation to Find Joy in God's Word

Let me give you a number of areas in which you should aim to experience joy in God's Word.

Find joy in its existence: Spurgeon said, "This great joy is sometimes aroused by the fact that there is a Word of God."[2] Yes, there is a book in which God reveals Himself. What a find! This takes us out of the fog and into the sunlight. We often take the existence of God's Word

---

1. Charles Bridges, *Psalm 119* (Edinburgh: Banner of Truth, 1974), 427.
2. Charles Spurgeon, *The Metropolitan Tabernacle Pulpit* (London: Banner of Truth, 1971), 28:50.

for granted, but try to imagine your life without it. Unless God had revealed himself we could never have known Him.

Find joy in its origin: Compare your lack of joy when receiving a letter from your utility company with the great joy of receiving a letter from an absent relative or friend. The origin of the letter determines how much pleasure it gives us. Therefore, when reading the Bible, the more we consciously realize that this is *God's* Word, that this is from *God* to us, that the ultimate author and speaker of these words is *God*, then the more joy there will be in reading it.

Find joy in its reliability: When we receive poorly written instructions with a new gadget or garden shed, it's not very inspiring, is it? The unreliability of the words makes us question the reliability of the gadget or the shed. But when we read the Bible, it's an immense joy to know that this book in our hands is unlike any other publication in the world. It is 100 percent truth: the truth, the whole truth, and nothing but the truth.

Find joy in its authority: In a world so full of conflicting opinions, ideas, and ethics; in a world where everyone is right and no one is wrong; in a world where everyone does what is right in his or her own eyes; in a world where the most solid words are "I think"—it's a joy to have God's Word come to us with ethical authority in its thou-shalts, thou-shalt-nots, and verily-verilys. Its certainty sweeps away all the doubts and questions.

Find joy in its clarity: Ever picked up a book and been totally frustrated at being unable to understand any or much of it? You won't get that frustration with the Bible. No, not everything in it is equally clear, but as the Westminster Confession of Faith puts it (1.7): "All things in Scripture are not alike plain in themselves, nor alike clear unto all: yet those things which are necessary to be known, believed, and observed for salvation are so clearly propounded and opened in some place of Scripture or other, that not only the learned, but the unlearned, in a due use of the ordinary means, may attain unto a sufficient understanding of them."

Find joy in its sufficiency: Although we might sometimes wish the Bible were bigger or more detailed and specific in some areas, God has given us enough inspired Scripture to know Him, to know what to believe about Him, and to know what to do in response. Our faith and duty is either expressly set forth or may be deduced from it. It lacks nothing essential to our faith and lives.

Find joy in its teaching: There's something about the human brain that loves to learn. The Word of God is an endless source of learning. We will never come to the point where we can say, "I know it all now." Not the most learned professor nor the most mature Christian in the world will ever exhaust its riches or plumb all its depths, and yet it's also suitable to teach children. As someone said, it's shallow enough for a child to paddle in and deep enough to challenge the biggest elephant.

Find joy in its grace: There could be no joy if this were a book of mere law, of dos, don'ts, guilt, condemnation, and judgment. But in finding its pages packed full of grace for the guilty and mercy for the miserable, we find great joy. Many of us can point to a text or passage that God used to open our eyes and give us new life. What profound joy fills our hearts and mouths when we read the words that God used to bring us alive from the dead, to open our eyes to the beauty of Christ.

Find joy in its cleansing: It's so good to come home to a refreshing shower if we've been working in a dirty yard or workshop. What an exhilarating feeling to step out of the shower and feel clean again. Similarly, as we read God's Word it cleanses us from the filth of this world and of our own hearts (Eph. 5:26). Sometimes we may not be conscious of it, we may not see immediate or obvious results, but it is happening, and we should rejoice in that deep inner cleansing.

Find joy in its strength: One of the words the psalmist uses for his "delight" in God's Word can be understood as "recreate." To paraphrase, "I *recreate* (lit. *delight*) myself in thy statutes" (Ps. 119:16). Sometimes we've faced difficulties in life and thought about giving up; then God's Word speaks into our lives and gives us renewed energy, motivation, drive, and enthusiasm. It gives us mental strength, spiritual strength, emotional strength, and even physical strength. We are strengthened to face difficulties, to serve, and to suffer (Ps. 119:50).

Find joy in its guidance: So many times we have wondered what we should do or where we should turn, and the Word of God has made the decision clear. What joy when the fog lifts and the way ahead is obvious.

Find joy in its correction: Sometimes God's Word corrects us; it grabs hold of us and points us in another direction. We may not like it at the time, but looking back we see the dangers and traps that we avoided.

Find joy in its warnings: We are all thankful for warning signs on the road, for example, those that warn us to slow us down lest we fly off the road at a dangerous bend. Similarly, God's warnings about hell should be a joy to us as they serve to keep us from danger and motivate us to show others the warnings too. We don't resent them but gratefully receive them from the God who knows far better than we do what is good for us.

Find joy in its promises: As Spurgeon said, "It is a good thing to mark your Bibles when you have received a promise. Mark the margin with T and P, and let it stand for "tried and proved."[3]

Find joy in its suitability: It's a constant wonder that God's Word is so suitable to so many different people in so many different places at so many different times in so many different circumstances. It just fits so well at critical times. As a pastor I'm continually amazed by how the Bible speaks to every situation. It is also so suitable for our culture with all the answers it needs for its problems.

Find joy in its communion: Unlike any other book, as we read God's Word we actually enter into communion with its author, God, through Christ by the Holy Spirit. As we read its pages the triune God comes out of the book and into our hearts. Spurgeon said, "When the Lord speaks to a man communion has in a measure begun.... This is God's side of a heavenly conversation."[4]

Find joy in its unity: One of the greatest pleasures in reading God's Word is to see how each Testament fits the other, how earlier books

---

3. Spurgeon, *Metropolitan Tabernacle*, 28:55.
4. Spurgeon, *Metropolitan Tabernacle*, 28:52.

shed light on later books and vice versa, and how it all fits together as part of one great and grand plan of redemption.

Find joy in its hope: The Bible is full of anticipation of a brighter and better future, holding out before us the prospect of the new heavens and the new earth in which dwell righteousness. It's like reading a travel brochure to the world's greatest destinations, and knowing that you are going to all of them at once.

Find joy in its songs: God's songs in the book of Psalms have been a delight to many Christians' souls throughout the centuries and up to this day. They thrill our hearts and carry our souls heavenwards.

Find joy in its realism: The Bible deals with the real world and with real problems. It doesn't deny them or downplay them. What are the really big moral issues of our day? Racism, injustice, homosexuality, child abuse, rape, abortion, etc. The Bible addresses all of these issues and more.

Find joy in its balance: Although the Bible warns us against worldliness, it also encourages a love for this world. The worldliness that it warns us against is accepting and following the norms, the values, the philosophies, and the sins of this world. But it also encourages us to value, cherish, care for, and enjoy this world, meaning this physical world that God created and still sustains.

Find joy in its worldview: The Bible gives us a lens through which to view the world, a framework with which to understand this world, its history, its present, and its future.

Find joy in its freshness: How many times we've come to read a portion of God's Word and it comes alive so that it feels like we've never read it before. The old becomes new; the old story comes with new power.

Find joy in its thanksgiving: One of the constant themes of God's Word is to "give thanks unto the LORD, for he is good" (Ps. 136:1). It's such a joy to trace every good and perfect gift back to God and to see every gift as a grace. Even science has found that gratitude is good for us. Some of its findings, published in books like *The Happiness Advantage*, *Flourish*, and *Optimal Functioning*, are:

- Consistently grateful people are more energetic, emotionally intelligent, forgiving, and less likely to be depressed, anxious, or lonely.[5]

- When researchers pick random volunteers and train them to be more grateful over a period of a few weeks, they become happier and more optimistic, feel more socially connected, enjoy better quality sleep, and even experience fewer headaches than control groups.[6]

- By noticing more kindness you'll experience more of it in your life. Counting kindness interventions involves taking daily tallies (mental or physical) of kind acts committed and witnessed; this activity has been shown to increase people's levels of positivity.[7]

- Gratitude encourages moral behavior and helps people cope with stress, trauma, and adversity.[8]

- It also inhibits negative comparisons with others and pushes out and replaces negative emotions.[9]

- When we express our gratitude to others, we strengthen our relationships with them.[10]

- Studies show that consistently grateful people are happier and more satisfied with their lives.

- They often feel more physically healthy and spend more time exercising.[11]

If that's what god-less thanksgiving can do for non-Christians, how much more can God-centered thanksgiving do for Christians!

Find joy in its pharmacy: The early church father, Basil, compared the Word of God to an apothecary's shop because when there is any

5. Shawn Achor, *The Happiness Advantage* (New York: Random House, 2010), 97–98.

6. Achor, *Happiness Advantage*, 97–98.

7. Jessica Colman, *Optimal Functioning: A Positive Psychology Handbook* (Amazon Digital Services, 2012), Kindle Locations 476–80.

8. Colman, *Optimal Functioning*, Kindle Location 493.

9. Colman, *Optimal Functioning*, Kindle Location 493.

10. Martin Seligman, *Flourish* (Simon & Schuster, 2011), Kindle Location 572–74.

11. Gretchen Rubin, *The Happiness Project* (New York: Harper, 2011), 202.

disease growing in the soul, there is a healing recipe to be found in the Bible.

These are twenty-five reasons to rejoice in God's Word, a rejoicing that pushes out delighting in lesser sources of joy, a rejoicing that is accompanied by reverence. Spurgeon said, "Unless we have deep awe of the word we shall never have high joy over it. Our rejoicing will be measured by our reverencing."[12]

An Example of Finding Joy in God's Word

"That's all very well," you might say, "but I'm feeling the opposite of joy. How do I get joy back again?" I want to give you an example of how God's Word can replace sad and pessimistic thoughts and feelings with happy and optimistic thoughts and feelings.

We start by noticing the Bible's teaching that what we think determines how we feel (Prov. 23:7; Rom. 12:2; Phil. 4:7–9). Scientific research backs this up. Studies have found that happiness is 50 percent genes, 10 percent circumstances, and 40 percent daily choices about what we think about and do.[13]

So if our thoughts determine our feelings, when we feel sad, depressed, discouraged, and unhappy, then we must focus on changing our thoughts. If we can change our thoughts for the better, then our feelings will also change for the better.

In Psalm 77, the Bible gives us a six-step process to enable us to change our thoughts with a view to changing our feelings. I want to present this to you by giving you six questions to ask, six questions in two groups of three. The first three help us *identify* our thoughts and recognize how they affect our emotions and behavior. The second three help us *challenge* our thoughts, change them, and so change our feelings and actions. In summary, we'll ask, "How did I get into this mood?" and then, "How do I get out of it?"

Turn to Psalm 77 where we read about Asaph's experience:

How did I get into this mood?

Step 1: What are the facts? Asaph's life situation is not defined in detail in Psalm 77. Asaph calls it "the day of my trouble" (v. 2), a deliberately general description that fits many life situations.

---

12. Spurgeon, *Metropolitan Tabernacle,* 28:49.
13. Sonja Lyubomirsky, *The How of Happiness* (New York: Penguin, 2007), 22.

Step 2: What does he think about these facts? When he considers the troubles in his life, Asaph concludes that God has rejected him, doesn't love him, has broken His promises, and has even changed in His character (vv. 7–9). As a result, he thinks that the past was great (v. 5), but the future is bleak and gloomy (v. 7).

Step 3: What is he feeling? He is inconsolably distressed by his trouble (v. 2) and overwhelmingly perplexed when he even thinks of God (v. 3). He feels abandoned by God and pessimistic about enjoying God's love and favor again (vv. 7–9).

How do I get out of this mood?

Step 4: Can he change the facts? There's no evidence that Asaph could change the facts or that his situation changed.

Step 5: Can he change his thoughts about the facts? At the end of verse 9, he pauses and takes time to be quiet, to still his soul and calm down. When he does that, new thoughts begin to form, transforming his perspective and outlook. He looks at the way he had been thinking and comes to the verdict, "This is my infirmity" (v. 10). This is his weakness. This is flawed and faulty thinking.

Then, in verses 10–12, he deliberately forces his mind to think new thoughts, to explore new areas for meditation. He says, "I'm not going to think like this anymore. I'm going to change my thinking habits and patterns." He firmly resolves:

- "I will remember the years of the right hand of the Most High.
- I will remember the works of the LORD:
- Surely I will remember thy wonders of old.
- I will meditate also of all thy work,
- and [I will] talk of thy doings" (vv. 10–12).

Notice that he refocuses his thinking upon God's powerful acts of providence through the centuries (vv. 13–20). Specifically, he notes how God sometimes leads His people through deep waters (v. 19) and sometimes through the wilderness (v. 20), but ultimately He leads them to the promised land (v. 20). For the believer, this is not just about thinking better; it's also about believing better. It involves thought patterns in the head, but it also involves faith patterns in the heart.

Step 6: What is he feeling now? Judging by Asaph's words in verses 13–20, there's a very different tone in his voice. He no longer questions God's existence, character, and providence but praises Him for His greatness, His wonders, His strength, and His redemption (vv. 13–15).

Instead of doubt, there is confidence; instead of pessimism, there is optimism; instead of vulnerability, there is security; instead of distress, there is comfort.

Asaph's facts have not changed, but his feelings have because, with the help of God's Word and works, he has changed his thoughts about the facts. We can see similar patterns of spiritual and emotional therapy in Psalms 42 and 43, Job 19, and Habakkuk 3.

Conclusion
I urge you to accept these exhortations to find joy in God's Word and, when you're down, to follow the example of God's Word to restore the joy of your salvation and find joy in God's Word again.

CHAPTER 10

Receiving and Doing the Word

James 1:21–25

Joel R. Beeke

The Bible is full of beautiful vignettes of godly people, and one of the most delightful is Tabitha, who was raised from the dead (Acts 9:36–42). The apostle Peter was near the town of Joppa when the disciples called for him. They were grieving the death of Tabitha, or Dorcas (both words mean "gazelle"; the first is Aramaic, and the second Greek). Peter knelt down by this woman's lifeless body, prayed, and then said, "Tabitha, arise." By the supernatural power of Christ, she was restored to life, opened her eyes, and sat up. The news spread, and many believed in the Lord because of this demonstration of His power and compassion.

However, we must not overlook another demonstration of God's glory, namely how it is revealed in the beauty of Tabitha's godly character manifested in her living out the Word she heard preached. The reason the church in Joppa so deeply mourned Tabitha's death was that she was "full of good works and almsdeeds," that is, acts of kindness to the poor (Acts 9:36). When Peter came in, he was greeted by the widowed disciples, their eyes full of tears. They showed him all the coats and garments Tabitha had made for them (Acts 9:39). She had spent her life caring for others at her own expense. It is no wonder that the people mourned her when she died and rejoiced when God raised her up again.

Too often when we think of great Christians, we think only of great theologians, preachers, missionaries, and other leaders of the church. To be sure, it is edifying for us to study their lives and writings. However, we too quickly forget the Tabithas of church history, the humble men and women who receive the Word and then devote themselves to doing what they hear: living righteously, serving and loving God and their neighbors. We need to remember that the great ones of God's kingdom are those who receive His Word and keep doing it in daily obedience until death takes them home.

We have read much in this book about the beauty and glory of the Word of God. In this closing chapter, we will consider the practical theme of receiving and doing the Word. James 1:21–22 says, "Wherefore lay apart all filthiness and superfluity of naughtiness, and receive with meekness the engrafted word, which is able to save your souls. But be ye doers of the word, and not hearers only, deceiving your own selves." The key words of this text are "receive" and "be doers," and these are also the two main points of my message.

This is a fitting text with which to close this book. James has just given his readers wise counsel, and now he says, "wherefore," or "therefore," receive the word and do it. In the same way, having read much about the beauty and glory of God's Word, I am saying to you, *therefore*, receive the Word and do it. However, I am also aiming at a larger target: I want to encourage you to begin or continue a lifetime of receiving God's Word and putting it into practice in your life, always remembering that, generally speaking, the best hearers make the best doers and the best doers make the best hearers.

Receive the Word of God into Your Minds and Hearts

The main verb of verse 21 is "receive."[1] This is not an option; it is a command. We have the responsibility to receive the Word of God, hear it, believe it, and apply it to our hearts and lives again and again by the Spirit's grace, just as we did when we were first converted.[2] As John Cotton said, "Feed upon the Word."[3] It is not enough to look at

---

1. The Greek verb translated "lay apart" (ἀποθέμενοι) is a participle modifying the command "receive" (ἀποθέμενοι). Bomberg and Kamell write, "It is technically incorrect to label this participle as imperatival per se, because it remains subordinate to a main verb later in the sentence; it is not a completely independent thought as with truly imperatival participles." Craig L. Blomberg and Mariam J. Kamell, *James*, Zondervan Exegetical Commentary on the New Testament, ed. Clinton E. Arnold (Grand Rapids: Zondervan, 2008), 87n25. Many thanks to Paul Smalley for his research assistance.

2. James primarily addresses those already born again (James 1:18), but the language of receiving the Word is used of conversion (Acts 8:14; 11:1; 17:11; 1 Thess. 1:6).

3. John Cotton, *The Way of Life* (London: M. F. for L. Fawne and S. Gellibrand, 1641), 432.

the food sitting on the plate; we must also put it in our mouths, chew it, and digest it thoroughly so that it becomes part of us.

Why Must We Receive the Word?

Reading the Bible and listening to sermons require work. Why is it absolutely crucial that listeners of the Word personally receive it? Why must you receive it, as Matthew Poole said, "not only into your heads by knowledge, but into your hearts by faith"?[4]

1. *We must receive the Word because it is the Word of God.* In the Bible, God talks to us. That should motivate us to receive everything it says with faith, fear, and reverence (Isa. 66:2). Paul writes in 1 Thessalonians 2:13, "For this cause also thank we God without ceasing, because, when ye received the word of God which ye heard of us, ye received it not as the word of men, but as it is in truth, the word of God."

2. *We must receive the Word because it is true.* In James 1:18 the Bible is called "the word of truth." The apostle Paul also often calls it "the word of truth" (2 Cor. 6:7; Eph. 1:13; Col. 1:5; 2 Tim. 2:15). It is not a collection of fables or human theories. Our Lord Jesus prayed, "Thy word is truth" (John 17:17). The Bible is able to fill us with truth that can make us truly wise unto salvation (Ps. 19:7; 2 Tim. 3:15).

3. *We must receive the Word because it works from the inside out.* James calls Scripture "the engrafted word." Spurgeon makes this expression come alive:

> When a graft is to be made, the first thing is to make a cut or gash. Nobody ever received the word of God into his heart to be engrafted there without being cut and wounded by the truth. It needs two wounds to make a graft; you wound the tree, and you wound that better tree which is to be grafted in. Is it not a blessed grafting when a wounded Savior comes into living contact with a wounded heart? When a bleeding heart is engrafted with a bleeding Savior? Engrafting implies that the heart is wounded and opened, and the living word is laid in and received with meekness into the bleeding, wounded soul of the man. There is the gash, and there is the space opened

---

4. Matthew Poole, *Commentary on the Whole Bible* (Peabody, Mass.: Hendrickson, n.d.), 3:883 (James 1:21).

thereby. Here comes the graft: the gardener must establish a union between the tree and the graft. This new life, this new branch, is inserted into the old stem, and they are to be livingly joined together. At first they are bound together by the gardener, and clay is placed about the points of junction; but soon they begin to grow into one another, and then only is the grafting effectual. This new cutting grows into the old, and it begins to suck up the life of the old, and change it so that it makes new fruit. That bough, though it be in the grafted tree, is altogether of another sort. Now we want the word of God to be brought to us after a similar fashion: our heart must be cut and opened, and then the word must be laid into the gash, till the two adhere, and the heart begins to hold to the word, to believe in it, to hope in it, to love it, to grow to it, to grow into it, and to bear fruit accordingly.... Oh, blessed grafting![5]

Literally, "the engrafted word" can also be translated as "the implanted word," that is, "the word that is planted within,"[6] like a seed planted and germinating in the soil. According to the parable of the sower, the soil is prepared by the prevenient grace and work of the Holy Spirit to receive the seed sown by those who preach it. James is not saying here that all people have some kind of innate, natural knowledge of God that saves, but rather that the Holy Spirit plants His Word in some people as they hear it preached.[7] When they receive the Word, it is implanted in the divinely prepared soil of the human heart.[8]

The Word of God is a living seed, full of eternal life and righteousness (1 Pet. 1:23; cf. 1 John 3:9). However, no seed will bear fruit if it merely lies on top of the dirt; it must penetrate the soil with its roots (Luke 8:13). God's Word will make no lasting change in our

---

5. Charles Spurgeon, *The Metropolitan Tabernacle Pulpit* (Pasadena, Texas: Pilgrim Publications, 1973), 31:357–58.

6. The Greek word ἔμφυτος appears only here in Scripture. It is derived from "in" (ἐν) and the verb "plant" (φυτεύω). On the metaphorical use of the latter for spiritual life, see Matt. 15:13; 1 Cor. 3:6–8.

7. Blomberg and Kamell, *James*, 88. The background for James's teaching here is not the innate word of reason in human nature according to Stoicism, but the sowing of the preached Word in people according Jesus Christ.

8. "Something inborn could have nothing to do with receiving." P. H. Davids, quoted in Ralph P. Martin, *James*, Word Biblical Commentary (Nashville: Thomas Nelson, 1988), 48–49.

lives if it touches us only in a superficial way. The Word must enter into us and abide with us by the Spirit, sending its spiritual influences like a root system throughout our minds, wills, and affections.[9] Calvin said, "It cannot be rightly received except it be implanted, or strike roots in us," becoming "united with our heart."[10] Only when the Word gets into our hearts do we truly benefit from it and bear fruit. James wrote primarily to people who were born again (James 1:18) and had the Word planted in them, but he reminds them that they must continue to receive the Word into their hearts that it might bear fruit in their lives.

4. *We must receive the Word because it is powerful.* James says in verse 21 that the Word is "able to save your souls." This Word is the truth that sets sinners free (John 8:32). Paul says that the Word of God "effectually worketh also in you that believe" (1 Thess. 2:13). Though the reading and preaching of the Bible does not have inherent power to save sinners, it is the instrument of the almighty God.[11] The Word is a fire that burns, a hammer that breaks, a sword that pierces, a lamp that illuminates, a seed that grows and bears fruit, and a bread that nourishes. You must receive the Word because it is the quick and powerful Word of God (Heb. 4:12), the sharp, two-edged sword of Christ (Rev. 1:16), and the sword of the Spirit (Eph. 6:17).

How Do We Receive the Word?
James says that to receive the Word, we must "lay apart all filthiness and superfluity of naughtiness." His words may be literally translated, "putting off all dirtiness and abundance of badness." Even the regenerated must struggle with a corrupt nature, or indwelling sin (James 1:14–15; 3:2, 6–8). We must take this sin off and throw it away as we would a filthy garment. Matthew Poole said that we must "not only restrain it, and keep it in; but put off, and throw it away as a filthy rag."[12] Or, like gardeners, we must "begin by rooting up noxious weeds" because "they are continually sprouting up," as Calvin

---

9. John 5:38; 8:37; 15:7; Col. 3:16; 1 John 1:8; 2:4, 14.
10. Calvin, *Commentaries on the Catholic Epistles* (Grand Rapids: Eerdmans, 1985), 294 (James 1:21).
11. Poole, *Commentary on the Whole Bible*, 3:883 (James 1:21).
12. Poole, *Commentary on the Whole Bible*, 3:883 (James 1:21).

said.[13] We cannot listen well to the Word unless we are willing to deal with our sins. We must listen with repentant hearts, viewing our sin as incredibly dangerous.

We must particularly deal with our unbelief and pride, our unwillingness to take wise advice, our covetousness and lustfulness, our tendency to assert our own opinions, and our anger that rises when someone speaks a hard word to us. Those are sins that James highlights in verses 19 and 21. Peter likewise writes in 1 Peter 2:1–2, "Wherefore laying aside all malice, and all guile, and hypocrisies, and envies, and all evil speakings, as newborn babes, desire the sincere milk of the word, that ye may grow thereby."

James tells us to receive the Word "with meekness." Meekness is not weakness, but a humble spirit that desires peace and is open to reason (James 3:13, 17). Calvin wrote, "By this word he means humility and the readiness of a mind disposed to learn."[14] Christ was commissioned to preach the gospel to the meek (Isa. 61:1). Meek people have a special promise of God's guidance and teaching, a promise that is given to no one else. Psalm 25:8–9 says, "Good and upright is the LORD: therefore will he teach sinners in the way. The meek will he guide in judgment: and the meek will he teach his way." To receive the Word with meekness is to listen with the fear of God and with hope in His mercy. It is to listen to the Word as the voice of God. Calvin said, "Wherever the gospel is preached, it is as if God himself came into the midst of us."[15]

A resolve to listen to the preached Word with humility and repentance has tremendous implications in three areas: how we read Scripture through the week, how we prepare for the preaching of the Word, and how we conduct ourselves during the preaching of the Word on the Lord's Day.

1. *Read the Word through the week.* The psalmist exclaimed, "O how love I thy law! It is my meditation all the day" (Ps. 119:97). A life of receiving the Word does not consist merely of one day of listening to sermons and six days of filling our minds with the world. That would leave us unprepared for the Lord's Day as well as injure our

---

13. Calvin, *Commentaries on the Catholic Epistles*, 294 (James 1:21).
14. Calvin, *Commentaries on the Catholic Epistles*, 294 (James 1:21).
15. John Calvin, *Commentary on a Harmony of the Evangelists*, trans. William Pringle (repr., Grand Rapids: Baker Books, 2003), 3:129 (Matt. 24:14).

spiritual life in a host of other ways. While the demands of our vocations and domestic responsibilities often limit how much time we can spend in Scripture through the week, we should meditate every day on the Bible. This is the way to know the Spirit's blessing and guidance in your life (Ps. 1:2).

The best way to maintain the discipline of daily meditation on Scripture is to read through the Bible. Reading the Bible may not be easy for you; it is a very large book written a long time ago, and parts of it may be hard to understand or seem irrelevant to your life. If we are going to be successful in reading the Bible, we must discipline ourselves to keep moving through Scripture.

We need God's grace to make progress in Bible reading and to benefit from it. Reading the Bible is not an end in itself; the ultimate end is communion with God through Jesus Christ. Therefore, grace is primary—most importantly, the grace of faith. Yet there are also some practical things you can do to help yourself read the Bible regularly and profitably. One of the most helpful books on reading Scripture was written by Richard Greenham titled *A Profitable Treatise, Containing a Direction for the Reading and Understanding of the Holy Scriptures.*[16] Greenham gave us eight helps for reading the Bible, each of which can be summarized in one word: diligence, wisdom, preparation, meditation, fellowship, faith, practice, and prayer.

We must exercise great *diligence* in reading Scripture, putting our energy into the task at hand and persisting in it. We ought to read the Bible with more diligence than men dig for hidden treasure, Greenham said. Diligence makes rough places plain, the difficult easy, and the unsavory tasty.

We must also use *wisdom* in our choices of what to read in the Bible, in what order, and at what time. Though we should read the entire Bible, it is not wise to spend most of our reading time on the hardest parts of Scripture. In terms of order, Greenham advised us to have a system that helps us get through the whole Bible, since only a

---

16. Richard Greenham, *A Profitable Treatise, Containing a Direction for the Reading and Understanding of the Holy Scriptures,* in *The Works of the Reverend and Faithfull Servant of Jesus Christ M. Richard Greenham,* ed. H. H. (London: by Felix Kingston for Robert Dexter, 1599), 389–97. For additional ideas on reading the Bible, see Joel R. Beeke, *How Teens Should Read the Bible* (Grand Rapids: Reformation Heritage Books, 2014).

whole Bible will make a whole Christian. As for time, no day should pass without reading the Bible.

Here is my counsel for daily Bible reading. Think about your day and choose the best time for reading your Bible. Read your Bible at that time, and don't let anything else usurp it. Find a place without distractions so that you can concentrate. Select a reading plan. There are lots of plans you can use, but a good one to start out with is one that takes you through the entire Bible in a year, or at most two years. Robert Murray M'Cheyne's plan has worked well for many people.[17]

Proper *preparation* is necessary. Without it, Scripture reading is seldom blessed. Preparation involves having a right attitude toward the Word so that we approach it with faith and reverence, determined like Mary to treasure God's Word and ponder it in our hearts (Luke 2:19). We prepare to approach Scripture with faith in Christ, looking to Him to open our intellect and understanding just as He did for His disciples long ago (Luke 24:45). And we prepare by stirring up a sincere desire in our hearts to be taught by God (Ps. 25:4–5) as we study His Word.

Duly prepared, we should read Scripture with *meditation*. Read slowly and thoughtfully. Some portions of Scripture, such as the book of Proverbs, need to be read slowly to allow time for meditation on each verse. It is better to read five verses from Proverbs with meditation and prayer than a hundred without.

One way to increase your meditation on the Bible is to memorize one verse each day from your reading. Reflect on that verse throughout the day. Memorization is particularly important when you are young. Most of the verses that I remember today are ones I memorized as a teenager. Fill your mind with Scripture now and it will benefit you for the rest of your life.

After reading, seek to engage in *fellowship* around the Word. Greenham called this a "conference" at which you talk with other believers about what you have read in the Bible. Others' insights will help you grow in knowledge and apply what you read. Proverbs 27:17 says it this way: "Iron sharpeneth iron; so a man sharpeneth the countenance of his friend."

---

17. *The Reformation Heritage KJV Study Bible,* gen. ed., Joel R. Beeke (Grand Rapids: Reformation Heritage Books, 2014), 2095–2103.

Scripture reading must also be mixed with *faith* in Jesus Christ. Faith is the key to truly profit from reading the Bible (Heb. 4:2). We should feed, strengthen, and exercise our faith through what we read. Martin Luther said, "To read the Holy Scriptures without faith in Christ is to walk in darkness."[18]

The goal of faith must be *practice*; we must read the Word with the goal of obeying it. For example, if you read Proverbs 3:5, "Trust in the LORD with all thine heart; and lean not unto thine own understanding," pause to ask yourself: Am I trusting in the Lord? What areas of my life am I not surrendering to Him? In what areas am I leaning on my own understanding? Then repent of your sins of unbelief and self-reliance, and turn to God in prayer for forgiveness and for strength to change. Trust in Him and in the wisdom of His Word, and cease to rely on your own instincts, opinions, and judgments.

Prayer is essential in all reading of Scripture, for we are dependent on the Holy Spirit to give us understanding and to show us how to apply the Word to our hearts and lives. Generally speaking, we don't receive the Spirit's help if we don't ask for it. Pray before you read the Bible, pray while you are reading it, and pray after you have read it. If we pray for nourishment from physical food at every meal, shouldn't we pray much more for spiritual nourishment from daily Bible reading?

Turn the Bible itself into petitions. Praying your way through the Psalms, for example, is very beneficial. Don Whitney's book, *Praying the Bible,* will be a great help to you in learning how to do this.[19]

A very useful tool to help you in your daily Bible reading is a good study Bible. While the notes and articles in a study Bible are not the pure and perfect word of God, they are the concise thoughts of wise Bible teachers, and the Spirit uses gifted teachers to bless the church (1 Cor. 12:4, 29). A study Bible collects brief thoughts from godly teachers to assist the reader.

Some parts of the Bible are hard to understand, as even the Bible acknowledges (2 Pet. 3:16). In the notes of a study Bible, you can find help for understanding obscure words and difficult sayings. You can

---

18. Martin Luther, *Lectures on Genesis, Chapters 45–50,* trans. Paul D. Pahl, in *Luther's Works,* ed. Jaroslav Pelikan and Walter A. Hansen (St. Louis: Concordia, 1966), 8:287.

19. Donald S. Whitney, *Praying the Bible* (Wheaton: Crossway, 2015).

study a book of the Bible in more depth by reading the introduction to that book and its notes, checking cross-references, and consulting the maps provided. If you want to learn more about a particular teaching of Scripture, you can read an article related to it in your study Bible, or the relevant part of a confession of faith or catechism cited in its appendices. Broaden your understanding of the Bible by reading an article on history. Some study Bibles have special sections on application that are particularly helpful for your devotions and family worship.[20]

If you cultivate the habit of daily reading and meditating on Holy Scripture with faith and prayer, then by God's grace you will draw near to Christ, experience a stronger faith, and live a more fruitful life of serving the Lord. A crucial part of receiving the Word of God is to read the Bible day by day, week by week, for a lifetime of learning. By shaping your mind with Scripture, you also receive maximum benefit from God's primary means of grace: the preaching of the Word.

2. *Prepare to hear the preached Word.* In writing about being a "hearer of the word" (James 1:23), James is primarily referencing preaching. In his day, copies of Scripture were written by hand on scrolls of paper or parchment. Such books were very expensive and few individual Christians could afford to own them. Literacy was rare and many Christians could not read Scripture for themselves. Hence, most Christians in those days were dependent on the public reading and preaching of the Word for their knowledge of Scripture. They had to be good "hearers of the Word" indeed!

The Lord Jesus admonishes us, "Take heed therefore how ye hear" (Luke 8:18). We are not to be passive listeners who merely wait for preaching to move us. If we are believers, we should be active listeners, engaging our minds and hearts to receive the truth of Holy Scripture; in fact, John Calvin asserted that we should be as involved in listening to the Word preached as the preacher is in proclaiming it! Together with the Spirit's sanctifying influence, we need to do our part in sanctification. Receiving the preached Word begins with

---

20. For the first study Bible that contains all of these elements, see *Reformation Heritage KJV Study Bible.*

preparing for services on the Lord's Day. As Thomas Manton said, "The instrument must be tuned ere it can make melody."[21]

There are five important ways to prepare for the preached Word:

First, before coming to God's house to hear His Word, prepare yourself and your family *with prayer*. As the Puritans were fond of saying, we should dress our bodies for worship and adorn our souls with prayer. Pray for the conversion of sinners, the edification of saints, and the glorification of God's triune name. Pray for children, teenagers, and the elderly. Pray for ears to hear and hearts to understand. Pray for yourself and your family, saying: "Lord, how real the danger is that we will not hear Thy Word as we should! Of the four kinds of hearers in the parable of the sower, only one kind heard properly. Focus our minds, Lord, to concentrate fully on Thy Word as it comes to us so that we may not hear the Word and yet perish. Give us faith to hear and profit from it. Let Thy Word have free course in our hearts. Let it be accompanied with light, power, and grace."

Pray that your minister will be empowered by the Holy Spirit to open his mouth boldly to make known the mysteries of the gospel (Eph. 6:19). Pray for an outpouring of the Spirit's life-giving, illuminating, and convicting power to work through God's ordinances in the fulfillment of His promises so your entire family is motivated for good (Prov. 1:23).

Second, stress the need for every family member to come with *a hearty appetite* for the Word. A good appetite promotes good digestion and growth. Peter says, "As newborn babes, desire the sincere milk of the word, that ye may grow thereby" (1 Pet. 2:2). A good appetite for the Word means having a tender, teachable heart (2 Chron. 13:7) that asks, "Lord, what wilt thou have me to do?" (Acts 9:6). It is foolish to expect a blessing if we come to worship with unprepared, unbelieving, hardened hearts.[22]

Third, discipline yourself and encourage your children to meditate on *the importance of the preached Word* as you enter God's house. The high and holy triune God of heaven and earth is meeting with you and your family to speak directly to you. Thomas Boston wrote,

---

21. Thomas Manton, *A Commentary on James*, Geneva (repr., Edinburgh: Banner of Truth, 1962), 145 (James 1:21).

22. Watson, *Body of Divinity*, 377.

"The voice is on earth, [but] the speaker is in heaven" (Acts 10:33).[23] What an awe-inspiring thought! Since the gospel is the Word of God rather than the word of man, come to church looking for God. Teach your children that ministers are God's ambassadors who bring you the Word of God (2 Cor. 5:20; Heb. 13:7). Manton wrote, "So much preparation there must be as will make the heart reverent. God will be served with a joy mixed with trembling."[24]

Remember that every sermon counts for eternity. Salvation comes through faith, and faith comes by hearing God's Word (Rom. 10:13–17). So every sermon is a matter of life and death (Deut. 32:47; 2 Cor. 2:15–16). The preached gospel will either lift us up to heaven or cast us down to hell. It will advance our salvation or aggravate our condemnation. It will draw us with the cords of love or leave us in the snares of unbelief. It will soften or harden us (Matt. 13:14–15), enlighten or darken our eyes (Rom. 11:10), open our hearts to Christ or shut them against Him. "The nearer to heaven any are lifted up by gospel preaching, the lower will they sink into hell if they heed it not," wrote David Clarkson.[25] "Take heed therefore how ye hear" (Luke 8:18)!

Furthermore, teach your children that on every Sabbath they are offered spiritual food and supplies for the coming week. The Puritans called the Sabbath "the market day of the soul."[26] As the Puritans went shopping for food each week, so we must stock up on spiritual goods for the week by listening to sermons, then meditating on them throughout the week to come. All of that must be reinforced with daily family worship and Christian living.

Fourth, remind yourself and your family periodically that as they enter the house of God they are *entering a battleground.* Many enemies will oppose your listening. Internally, you may be distracted by worldly cares and employments, lusts of the flesh, a cold heart, or a critical spirit. Externally, you may be distracted by behavior or the dress of others, noises, or people moving about. Satan opposes your listening to God's Word, knowing that if you truly hear it, he

---

23. Boston, *Works,* 2:28.
24. Manton, *James,* 146 (James 1:21).
25. Clarkson, *Works,* 1:430–31.
26. James T. Dennison, Jr., *The Market Day of the Soul: The Puritan Doctrine of the Sabbath in England, 1532–1700* (Morgan, Penn.: Soli Deo Gloria, 2001).

will lose you. So Satan tries to disturb you before the sermon begins, distracts you during the sermon, and tries to erase the sermon from your mind as soon as it is finished. Like a bird plucking away a newly sown seed, Satan attempts to snatch the Word from your mind and heart so that it cannot take root. Resist him by the power of Christ.[27]

Fifth, pray that you might come with *a loving, expectant faith* (Ps. 62:1, 5). Come pleading God's promise that His word will not return to Him void, that is, not having accomplished the purpose for which He sent it forth (Isa. 55:10–11). Pray that you and your family might be able to say with the psalmist in Psalm 119, "Thy word is very pure: therefore thy servant loveth it" (v. 140), and to love God's testimonies "exceedingly" (v. 167), more than gold (v. 127), and to the point where they nearly consume you (v. 20). The psalmist's love for God's Word is so fervent that he would meditate upon it "all the day" (v. 97). In dependence on the Spirit, cultivate such love for the Word of God in yourself and in your children.

As the Holy Spirit blesses such preparations, we will find ourselves ready to receive the message God is giving us through the ministry of the Word. However, our work does not end with preparation. We must continue to exercise ourselves when the sermon begins.

3. *Listen to the preached word.* When you sit before the preacher, listen in six ways:

First, listen *with an understanding, tender conscience.* Jesus' parable of the sower (Matt. 13:3–23; Mark 4:1–20; Luke 8:4–15) describes four types of listeners, all of whom hear the same Word. Some hearers are indifferent and untouched by what they hear. Some hear, but only superficially; they soon fall away. Others hear, but are distracted and burdened by the cares of life and the deceitfulness of riches; they, too, fall away. Thankfully some are prepared to receive the Word, and it takes root in their hearts and brings forth much fruit in their lives. The understanding, fruitful listener applies the gospel teaching he hears on Sunday to his conscience and life throughout the week. He believes with his heart that if Jesus Christ has sacrificed everything for him, nothing is too difficult to surrender in grateful obedience to Christ. Before all else, he seeks the kingdom of God

---

27. *Puritan Sermons 1659–1689* (Wheaton, Ill.: Richard Owen Roberts, 1981), 4:187.

(Matt. 6:33). Grace reigns in his heart. He brings forth fruit, "some an hundredfold, some sixty, some thirty" (Matt. 13:23).

Second, listen *attentively* to the preached Word. Luke 19:48 reports that "all the people were very attentive to hear him," that is, to hear Christ as He taught daily in the temple. Literally translated, the text says, "they hung upon him, hearing." Because the Lord had opened Lydia's heart, she "attended" or "turned her mind" to the things spoken by Paul (Acts 16:14). Such attentiveness involves banishing wandering thoughts, dullness of mind, and drowsiness (Matt. 13:25). It regards a sermon as a matter of life and death (Deut. 32:47).

Third, we must not listen to sermons as spectators but *as participants*. Good listening is hard work; it involves worshiping God continuously. An attentive listener also responds quickly—whether with faith, repentance, resolution, determination, or praise—and God is honored in this. The Westminster Confession of Faith (14.2) summarizes such listening this way:

> By this faith, a Christian believeth to be true whatsoever is revealed in the Word, for the authority of God Himself speaking therein; and acteth differently upon that which each particular passage thereof containeth; yielding obedience to the commands, trembling at the threatenings, and embracing the promises of God for this life, and that which is to come. But the principal acts of saving faith are accepting, receiving, and resting upon Christ alone for justification, sanctification, and eternal life, by virtue of the covenant of grace.

Fourth, listen *for life-changing ideas*. As you listen to the Word of God, ask yourself: how does God want me to be different because of what I am hearing in this sermon? Ask what truths you are learning that He wants you to believe. And ask how He wants you to put those truths into practice. In every sermon you hear—even those on the most basic gospel themes—God offers you truths to believe and put into practice. Pray for grace to work at listening. Manton said, "The servants of God come with a mind to obey; they do but wait for the discovery of their duty."[28]

Fifth, listen *with the submission of true faith*. As James 1:21 says, "Receive with meekness the engrafted word." This kind of listening

---

28. Cf. Ps. 123:2. Manton, *James*, 150 (James 1:21).

involves "a willingness to hear the counsels and reproofs of the word," Watson said.[29] Through this kind of faith, the Word is engrafted into the soul and produces "the sweet fruit of righteousness."[30]

"The whole Word is the object of faith," wrote Manton. All the parts of the Bible "have their use: the histories to make us wary and cautious; the doctrines to enlighten us with a true sense of God's nature and will; the precepts to direct us, and to try and regulate our obedience; the promises to cheer and comfort us; the threatenings to terrify us, to run anew to Christ, to bless God for our escape, and to add spurs to our duty."[31]

Finally, listen *with humility and self-examination*. Ask yourself: Do I humbly examine myself under the preaching of God's Word, trembling under the weight of it (Isa. 66:2)? Do I cultivate a meek and submissive spirit, receiving God's truth as a student while being intimately aware of my own depravity? Do I seriously examine myself under preaching, listening for my own benefit rather than thinking of how the Word may apply to others? Do I pray that the Spirit may apply His Word, as Robert Burns put it, to my "business and bosom"?[32]

If a doctor tells you what to do to maintain your health or that of your children, you should listen carefully so that you can follow his directions. When the heavenly Physician gives you divine directions for your soul, should you not listen every bit as carefully so that you can follow God's instructions for your life?

The Holy Spirit calls you through James 1:21 to *receive the Word*. You have a solemn responsibility and happy opportunity to have this precious seed planted in your heart. If the Word of God dwells in you, it can be said of you as it was said of Richard Sibbes: "Heaven was in him before he was in heaven."[33]

---

29. Watson, *Body of Divinity*, 377.

30. Watson, *Body of Divinity*, 378.

31. Thomas Manton, *The Life of Faith* (Ross-shire, Scotland: Christian Focus, 1997), 223–24.

32. Robert Burns, "Introductory Essay," in *The Works of Thomas Halyburton* (London: Thomas Tegg, 1835), xiv.

33. Quoted in Stapleton Martin, *Izaak Walton and His Friends* (London: Chapman & Hall, 1903), 174.

All of this is summarized well by Puritan preachers who explained how the preaching of the Word effected personal transformation.[34] The Westminster Larger Catechism summarizes their advice: "It is required of those that hear the word preached, that they attend upon it with diligence, preparation, and prayer, examine what they hear by the Scriptures, receive the truth with faith, love, meekness, and readiness of mind, as the word of God; meditate, and confer of it in their hearts, and bring forth the fruit of it in their lives."[35]

It is glorious to think of having the living seed of God's Word planted in our souls so that it brings forth fruit in our lives. Only then do we taste of its goodness. As James exhorts us, we must not only hear the Word, but do it.

Be a Doer of the Word of God

The Holy Spirit says in James 1:22, "Be ye doers of the word, and not hearers only, deceiving your own selves." If we are not doers, then we have never truly been hearers and receivers. Manton said, "The doers of the word are the best hearers.... That knowledge is best which is most practical, and that hearing is best which endeth

---

34. Samuel Annesley, "How May We Give Christ a Satisfying Account [of] Why We Attend upon the Ministry of the Word?," in *Puritan Sermons 1659–1689, Being Morning Exercises at Cripplegate* (Wheaton, Ill.: Richard Owen Roberts, 1981), 4:173–98; David Clarkson, "Hearing the Word," in *The Works of David Clarkson* (Edinburgh: Banner of Truth, 1988), 1:428–46; Thomas Manton, "The Life of Faith in Hearing the Word," in *The Complete Works of Thomas Manton* (London: James Nisbet, 1873), 15:154–74; Jonathan Edwards, "Profitable Hearers of the Word," in *The Works of Jonathan Edwards, Volume 14, Sermons and Discourses 1723–1729*, ed. Kenneth P. Minkema (New Haven: Yale, 1997), 243–77; Thomas Senior, "How We May Hear the Word with Profit," in *Puritan Sermons,* 2:47–57; Thomas Watson, *A Body of Divinity* (Grand Rapids: Sovereign Grace Publishers, 1972), 377–80; Thomas Boston, *The Complete Works of the Late Rev. Thomas Boston* (Wheaton, Ill.: Richard Owen Roberts, 1980), 2:427–54; Thomas Shepard, "Of Ineffectual Hearing the Word," in *The Works of Thomas Shepard* (Ligonier, Penn.: Soli Deo Gloria, 1992), 3:363–84.

Several nineteenth-century sources stand in the Puritan tradition: John Newton, "Hearing Sermons," in *The Works of John Newton* (Edinburgh: Banner of Truth, 1985), 1:218–25; John Elias, "On Hearing the Gospel," in *John Elias: Life, Letters and Essays* (Edinburgh: Banner of Truth, 1973), 356–60; Edward Bickersteth, *The Christian Hearer* (London: Seeleys, 1853). The last is very thorough and helpful.

35. Westminster Shorter Catechism (Q. 160), in *Westminster Confession of Faith* (Glasgow: Free Presbyterian Publications, 1997), 253.

in practice."[36] Christians are not to be mere listeners but people of action who translate their faith into works of obedience.

Why Must We Be Doers of the Word, Not Just Hearers?

People may come to church and enjoy preaching in the same way they would enjoy listening to a singer at a concert, but walk away unchanged for the better (Ezek. 33:32). Tragically, those who hear the Word of God but do not obey it often become self-righteous and judgmental.[37]

1. *We must be doers because if we are only hearers, we lie to ourselves.* James says that if you are "hearers only," you are "deceiving your own selves" (1:22b). This is deeply ironic, for such hearers often think they are full of the truth. They may have heads full of knowledge but their hearts are full of lies. They assume they are blessed by their hearing of the Word when in fact that blessing is only reserved for doers of the Word. The non-doer may be able to tell others the truth, but he refuses to tell himself the truth. What a tragic situation! The only way to really embrace the truth is to do it. We must be, as our forefathers often quipped, "walking Bibles."

2. *We must be doers because it is useless—worse than useless—to hear and do nothing.* James goes on in verses 23–24 to describe a man who looks into a mirror, sees his reflection for a moment, then goes on his way, forgetting what he has seen. Nothing has changed and the man is no better for what he has seen. If we are hearers only, we are in worse condition than those who were not hearers at all for, as Jesus says in Luke 10:14–15, it shall be more tolerable for Tyre and Sidon in the day of judgment than for places like Capernaum to which the revelation of the gospel has been given—more tolerable for those who went to eternity without ever hearing one syllable of the gospel than for those who have heard the gospel constantly and who have not been influenced by it. We have to take care lest that "doing nothing" should lead to our eternal condemnation.

Thomas Manton spoke of a foolish workman who is content to have tools but never does anything with them.[38] Our Lord Jesus

---

36. Manton, *James*, 153 (James 1:22).
37. Matt. 7:1–5; 15:1–9; 23:1–3; Rom. 2:1–2, 13, 17–24.
38. Manton, *James*, 153 (James 1:22).

warns against such folly in Matthew 7:26–27, "Every one that heareth these sayings of mine, and doeth them not, shall be likened unto a foolish man, which built his house upon the sand: and the rain descended, and the floods came, and the winds blew, and beat upon that house; and it fell: and great was the fall of it." People would walk by and think, "What a fool! He built a house with no foundation— just sand!" Likewise, we are fools when we listen to the words that call us to faith and obedience and tell us of eternal consequences, but do nothing.

3. *We must be doers because obedience is the pathway of freedom.* In verse 25, James calls the Word of God "the perfect law of liberty." The wicked think that God's Word is a chain to hold them in bondage (Ps. 2:1–3), but true believers know the Word of Jesus Christ sets us free (John 8:31–32). Poole wrote, "It shows the way to the best liberty, freedom from sin, the bondage of the ceremonial law, the rigour of the moral [law], and from the wrath of God; and likewise the way of serving God freely and ingenuously [sincerely] as children; and because, being received into the heart, it is accompanied with the Spirit of adoption who works this liberty (2 Cor. 3:17)."[39]

When the believer receives grace to believe in Christ and experiences Jesus Christ as the end of the law to everyone that believes in terms of justification, he then embraces God's perfect law in light of the perfect Savior unto sanctification. He views God's law through the pierced body of Jesus Christ who died for him and becomes heartily willing to obey all the commandments of God. Being under the liberty of grace he feels more deeply his subjection to divine law as the rule of life for, as Paul says, he is "not without law to God, but under the law to Christ" (1 Cor. 9:21). Because all aspects of the believer's relationship to God are *in* Christ and *to* Christ, the law is for him the "law of liberty."

Out of gratitude to God Triune, he now desires to obey the law. He understands now how the Puritans could speak of "the grace of law" while simultaneously maintaining that salvation is only by grace.

Such liberty makes Christ's yoke easy. Then the believer experiences liberty from the yoke of sin—its guilt, consequences, and dominion—as well as liberty from Satan and from the world. The

---

39. Poole, *Commentary on the Whole Bible*, 3:883 (James 1:25).

bondage of the gospel is the sweet bondage of love, for it is the love of God shed abroad in the souls that binds the sinner willingly back to God.

Such freedom, being obedient freedom, is, as Calvin put it, both "a free servitude and a serving freedom." Only "those who serve God are free. We obtain liberty in order that we may more promptly and more readily obey God."[40]

4. *We must not be hearers only, because only doers are blessed by God*, as James declares in verse 25: "this man shall be blessed in his deed." God's blessing is the crown He places on those whose lives bear fruit in response to the Word. Honor and life belong to those who continue or persevere in doing God's Word (James 1:12). This is not legalism, but recognition that practical works of obedience are the fruits and graces of a living faith in Christ, as James expounds in chapter 2. Calvin wrote, "The doer is he who from the heart embraces God's word and testifies by his life that he really believes, according to the saying of Christ, 'Blessed are they who hear God's word and keep it' (Luke 11:28), for he shows by the fruits" that the word is implanted in his soul.[41]

How Do We Become Doers of the Word?

To become a doer of the Word, you must first be born again. Only God can give you a heart of faith and obedience. James writes in James 1:18, "Of his own will begat he us with the word of truth, that we should be a kind of firstfruits of his creatures." Those who are regenerated by God then become doers of the Word. John writes in 1 John 2:29, "If ye know that he is righteous, ye know that every one that doeth righteousness is born of him."

However, those who are regenerated by God must grow in practicing the Word. You may not rest in your past conversion but press on in spiritual growth. Every time you hear the Word you must exercise obedience as a doer of the Word. "HEED" the Word by following this simple acronym: be a

---

40. John Calvin, *Institutes of the Christian Religion*, ed. John T. McNeill, trans. Ford Lewis Battles (Philadelphia: Westminster Press, 1960), 2.7.10.

41. Calvin, *Commentaries on the Catholic Epistles*, 296–97 (James 1:22).

- Humble hearer;
- Earnest hearer;
- Eager hearer;
- Doing hearer.

Here is some practical counsel on how to grow as a doer of the Word.

1. *Familiarize yourself with the truths you have heard.* Meditate in private on what you heard in public. The Westminster Directory for Public Worship advises parents to engage in "repetition of sermons, especially by calling their families to an account of what they have heard."[42] When you come home from church, speak to your children about the sermon you have heard in an edifying, practical manner. Talk about the sermon in words that your youngest child will understand.

Encourage your children to take notes on the sermon. My wife and I have trained our children since they were age seven to take notes. After the last service each Sabbath, we read through those notes as a family and talk our way through the sermons. Sometimes the discussions help our children more than the sermons do. Even when conversation does not produce the desired results, continue this review of Sabbath sermons. It is better to fall short than not to attempt at all. One sermon properly meditated upon with the assistance of the Holy Spirit will do more good than dozens of unapplied and quickly forgotten sermons. Thomas Watson said we should not let sermons run through our minds like water through a sieve. "Our memories should be like the chest of the ark, where the law was put," he wrote.[43]

2. *Pray over what you have heard.* Bring back to God in your prayers what He has given you in the Word. Joseph Alleine said one way to remember the preached Word is to "come from your knees to the sermon, and come from the sermon to your knees."[44] An elderly woman once told me, "I take thorough sermon notes. When I bow my knees on Sunday evening, I put my notes in front of me, underline those things that I should strive to put into practice, and then pray through

---

42. *Westminster Confession of Faith*, 386.
43. Watson, *Body of Divinity*, 378.
44. Joseph Alleine, *A Sure Guide to Heaven* (Edinburgh: Banner of Truth, 1999), 29.

them one at a time." Imitate this woman, and encourage your children to do the same.

3. *Engage your affections with the truths you have heard.* Take what you have understood and use it to stir up hatred for sin, love for Christ, and compassion for people. We cannot be passive in the spiritual life. Yes, it is true that God must work within us; but when God works, He move us to work. Part of our work as hearers and doers of the Word is to stir ourselves up. Martyn Lloyd-Jones said,

> The main art in the matter of spiritual living is to know how to handle yourself. You have to take yourself in hand, you have to address yourself, preach to yourself, question yourself. You must say to your soul, 'Why art thou cast down'.... Exhort yourself, say to yourself: 'Hope thou in God'.... And then you must go on to remind yourself of God, Who God is, and what God is and what God has done, and what God has pledged Himself to do.[45]

4. *Make specific resolutions of how you intend to obey the Word.* Too often application fails because it remains too general and never touches the details of life. "I will be a more loving husband" is really not a decision to do anything. Better would be, "I will take my wife out to eat next week, ask her how I could be a more loving husband, and start to work on whichever point *she* feels is more important." Don't let the day end until you write down a specific resolution or two of how you will be a doer of the Word you have heard.

5. *Tell a godly friend how the sermon applies to you.* This practice not only encourages edifying conversation on the Lord's Day, but it also gives you more motivation to follow through. You are more likely to remember what you say than what you think. You and your friend may then talk about how you can work out your obedience practically. Your friend may ask you next week what you did. Better yet, he may pray for you. Furthermore, you might be surprised that after you tell your friend how the sermon applies to you he might say, "I think I should do the same thing as you!"

---

45. D. Martyn Lloyd-Jones, *Spiritual Depression: Its Causes and Its Cure* (Grand Rapids: Eerdmans, 1965), 21.

6. *Build your obedience to God's law upon your faith in God's gospel.* Remember that the order of the Christian life is never obedience first, but faith first, then obedience. The apostle Paul says, "I live by the faith of the Son of God, who loved me, and gave himself for me" (Gal. 2:20). Obey by faith in Christ. Self-reformation by self-will cannot produce anything more than superficial change. The law of God can convict you of sin and direct you in the way of duty, but it cannot give you a heart to fulfill it. Only the Holy Spirit can do this, working faith in your heart through the gospel of Jesus Christ. So let your obedience be the obedience of faith, grasping hold of Christ as the Prophet, Priest, and King to teach, forgive, and rule you. Then move ahead to action, leaning on the Holy Spirit, and not on your own wisdom or willpower.

7. *Put the sermon into action and persevere in obedience and good works.* A sermon is not over when the minister says "Amen." Rather, that is when the true sermon begins. In an old Scottish story, a wife asked her husband if the sermon was done. "No," he replied, "it has been said, but it has yet to be done." Always seek to live out the sermons you hear, even if that means denying yourself, bearing your cross, or suffering for the sake of righteousness.

8. *Use the Word preached and read to put into practice the task of evangelizing others.* Let the Word change you and then let it work through you to reach others and draw them to Christ. There is no more powerful or persuasive witness than the testimony of a changed, renewed life. True listening includes applying the Word of God. If you do not practice the Word of God after you have heard it, you have not truly listened to God's message.

Conclusion

As God created seed to produce fruit, so God sends forth His Word to produce sanctified people who do good works (Isa. 55:10–11). This mission calls us to be hearers of the Word and doers of the Word. Poole said, "Receive the word by faith into your hearts, and bring forth the fruit of it in your lives."[46]

---

46. Poole, *Commentary on the Whole Bible*, 3:883 (James 1:21).

Are you an active hearer of God's Word? Are you a diligent doer of the Word? Or do you listen to sermons half-heartedly? If the latter is true, repent of your sin and begin to actively listen to His Word. It is not enough for you to attend church any more than sitting in the doctor's office will heal your disease! You must be an active hearer and doer of the Word. Watson warned lukewarm listeners: "Dreadful is their case who go loaded with sermons to hell."[47] Your knowledge will only increase your condemnation.

What kind of a hearer of the Word of God are you? Consider seriously that there are many kinds of false hearers. Spurgeon spoke of self-deceived hearers, superficial hearers, hasty hearers, forgetful hearers, admiring hearers, affectionate hearers, and attached hearers, all of whom are unfruitful and unblessed hearers because they are not receiving and doing hearers.[48]

On the other hand, you who walk with God in the pathways of blood-bought holiness, remember that our Lord blesses you, saying, "If ye know these things, happy are ye if ye do them" (John 13:17). Thank God for all that you receive from sermons. Give glory to God when you are able to put God's Word into practice. Honor Him for every speck of love and obedience in your life. And press on doing good, knowing that by the light of your works, people will see the beauty of God and come to worship Him. "And many people shall go and say, Come ye, and let us go up to the mountain of the LORD, to the house of the God of Jacob; and he will teach us of his ways, and we will walk in his paths: for out of Zion shall go forth the law, and the word of the LORD from Jerusalem" (Isa. 2:3).

If, by the Spirit's grace, you act on what you have read and bring forth the fruit of it in your lives, we can call this book a success. May God help us to be not only hearers but also doers of His clear, authoritative, sufficient, inspired, infallible, inerrant, and joyous Word of life that remains full of wonder to believers.

---

47. Watson, *Body of Divinity*, 380.
48. Spurgeon, *Metropolitan Tabernacle Pulpit*, 25:199–201.